MACMILLAN CAR

Ian McDonald
Selected Poems

EDITED BY
Edward Baugh

MACMILLAN
CARIBBEAN

Macmillan Education
Between Towns Road, Oxford, OX4 3PP
A division of Macmillan Publishers Limited
Companies and representatives throughout the world

www.macmillan-caribbean.com

ISBN: 978-0-230-02871-5

Text © Ian McDonald 1988, 1992, 1994, 2003, 2008
Design and illustration © Macmillan Publishers Limited 2008

Design by Mike Brain Graphic Design Ltd
Typeset by Expo Holdings
Cover design by Clare Webber
Cover photo: Ian McDonald

The publisher and author wish to thank the following rights holders for the use of
copyright material:

Peepal Tree Press for the following poems by Ian McDonald:

Between Silence and Silence (Peepal Tree Press, 2003)
Praise Song for Mary, My Father's Prayer Book, Page 44, Gifts for a Farewell,
The Weather in Shanty Town, Shadows Will Hide the Sun, White Cathedrals,
Greeneyes, Betrothal, Bread and Fish Hooks, Beaucaillou, Seen Through Closed
Eyes, Rain, Archive, MacArthur's Life, Sing-Song's Place, Canticle of the Main Street
Madman, Mr Perfection, Spinster Ganteaume and the Birth of Poetry, Tree of
Dreams, Massa Day Done, Meeting Once a Year at Britnell's, The Pear-Wood Cup,
Between Silence and Silence There Should Be Only Praise.

Jaffo the Calypsonian (Peepal Tree Press, 1994)
Temple Bullock, Rumshop Girl, Bright Cockerel, Mais of Jamaica, Decorated for a
Kiss, Young Harpooner, Lonely Near Educated Water, The Legend of Mangamuch
and La Cour Harpe, Walking on Lily Leaves, Jaffo the Calypsonian, Pineapple
Woman, Mystic at the Nightclub Miramar, The Stick-Fighters, The Four Knives of
Freeman, the Cane-cutter, Indian Love Statement, The Seine-Pullers, Statement to
God, Georgetown Children, Hispaniola, Railwaymen, Pelting Bees, Yusman Ali,
Charcoal Seller, Poem on a Black Stone, On an Evening Turned to Rain, State of the
Nation, Drunk, A White Man Considers the Situation.

Uncollected
Any Poem, Birdsong, Silence, Strange Plot, What It Was Like Once Forever.
and Peterloo Poets for all the other poems.

If any copyright holders have been omitted, please contact the publishers who will
make the necessary arrangements at the first opportunity.

Printed and bound in Hong Kong

2012 2011 2010 2009 2008
10 9 8 7 6 5 4 3 2 1

Contents

Early to Mid-1980s

Late 1980s and After

Introduction

When Ian McDonald's 'Jaffo the Calypsonian', his first published poem, appeared in *Bim*, No. 22 (June 1955), it struck a new and distinctive chord in West Indian poetry. This chord was to be rehearsed, at relatively long intervals, also in *Bim*, over the next few years, in poems such as 'The Stick-Fighters', 'The Seine-Pullers', 'The Legend of Mangamuch and La Cour Harpe' and 'The Four Knives of Freeman, the Cane-Cutter'. These poems celebrated the single-minded strength of personality of ordinary folk – calypsonian, fisherman, stick-fighter – their pride and pleasure in doing well what they did, whether at work or at play. The life force they express is radiant, even when it is a matter of bitter defiance of the bad hand that life has dealt them, as in the case of 'Yusman Ali, Charcoal Seller', who "farts at the beauty of the rain-dipped moon". "His spit blazes in the sun. An emperor's bracelet shines."

The characteristic form and style of these poems were also distinctive. They used a very long line, unrhymed and rhythmically flat, tending toward prose and formatted in simple, definitive sentences, with inventive turns of phrase and bold, clearly drawn images, featuring juxtaposition of strong colours. Expression and subject-matter combine to produce a narrative-descriptive effect that suggests the possibility of folk epic. There is also at times an intensely lyrical quality to the description. This quality is concentrated in sparkling or heart-hurting lyrics such as 'Decorated for a Kiss', 'Statement to God', 'Pelting Bees' and 'Poem on a Black Stone'. Also, in contrast to the long-line, flat-rhythm pieces are a few poems in rhyming couplets of strongly accented tetrameter – 'Pineapple Woman', 'Hispaniola', 'Georgetown Children' – a songlike form that suggests the popular ballad. All in all, these poems brought West Indian folk and folkways definitively into the scribal tradition of West Indian poetry, in effect complementing the work of the Jamaican performance poet Louise Bennett.

The distinguishing trends of McDonald's path-finding poems of the 1950s and 1960s were developed, with variations, in his subsequent work. For instance, the long line of plain statement is, in some of the best of the later pieces, more rhythmically accented, with judicious introduction of occasional rhyme. So '"Hangman" Cory' makes a nice comparison with 'The Legend of Mangamuch and La Cour Harpe'.

Interestingly, his poems of the 1950s and 1960s remained mostly uncollected for a very long time, until the publication of *Jaffo the Calypsonian* (Peepal Tree Press, 1994). Eleven had appeared in *Poetry Introduction* 3 (Faber & Faber, 1975). These and another eleven were published in the chapbook *Selected Poems* (The Labour Advocate, 1983). McDonald's first major collection was *Mercy Ward* (Peterloo Poets, 1988), which won the Guyana Prize for Literature in 1992. It consisted of poems written in the first half of the 1980s, after a decade of creative drought. Then came the *Essequibo* collection (Peterloo Poets & Story Line Press, 1992), consisting of poems written in the late 1980s. Then, after *Jaffo*, came his latest collection, *Between Silence and Silence* (Peepal Tree Press, 2003), containing poems written mostly after 1990. This collection was awarded the Guyana Prize for Literature in 2004. Given the publication date of *Jaffo*, it will be evident that the sequence of publication of McDonald's four major collections does not match the chronology of composition of the poems, which chronology the grouping of the present selection broadly indicates.

The *Mercy Ward* sequence is represented in the group of poems headed "The early to mid-1980s", with the exception of the last four. The *Mercy Ward* poems came out of the poet's observation of the patients in a Georgetown hospital "for the poorest of the poor" ('The Cancer'). Here again we see McDonald's concern for the so-called common people, and how his social conscience expresses itself in terms of his recognition of the force of life and personality in the individual, even the lowliest and most socially deprived. The poem which started and inspired the sequence was 'God's Work', about a man, "Mister Edwards" as he called him, who had been the poet's gardener and eventually his friend for many years, and who died a slow, agonising death. The gut-wrenching pain of the experience is both deepened and balanced by the strength, stoicism and faith of this strong man reduced to a remnant of himself, and by the poem's closing, cuttingly ironic comment: "God should play more."

Not surprisingly for McDonald, *Mercy Ward* is a portrait gallery of characters. For instance, there is Hubertus Jones, schoolmaster of the old school, "Who taught a full class [in Mercy Ward] and set them homework," and "confirmed in writing to Central Board / all that was wrong in Mercy Ward" ('The Last Classroom of Hubertus Jones'). There is "hook-nosed Amoroso", who, demanding "the right / to better food", "had a victory" when he is "Served, on special china, / Red sweet peppers / Stuffed with garlic crab" ('Sweet Pepper Sunday'). When a member of the British Royal Family, apparently Princess Margaret, visits the hospital, "old Mangru, not known for being difficult" has his moment of glory, when he not only refuses to speak to the royal visitor, but, when she had gone just a little way beyond his bed, "Gave forth the loudest fart you ever, ever heard" ('Royal Visit'). The humour gives an additional dimension to the life force that asserts itself in the face of despair and death. Hubertus Jones, Amoroso, Mangru – the names themselves indicate something of Guyana's racial diversity, which McDonald's poetry represents well.

Memorable characters also feature in McDonald's next two collections: *Essequibo* and *Between Silence and Silence*. The ones we meet in *Essequibo* are strange, sometimes eccentric, reclusive, appropriate to and influenced by the mysterious, intense, primal domain of the great Essequibo river. "Here men you meet are strange wayfarers", like the Englishman, university graduate, irredeemably possessed by his quest for the mythical Amazons ('Explorer'), or the old priest with his thousands of scholarly books, "brought from Heidelberg and Rome", now "worm-holed, rat-eaten, damp-decayed", and his "marvellous notebooks two thousand pages long" which the world will never read ('Scholar'). Then there is the pale Norseman, who "runs a rumshop" at the "frontier river-town, deep in forest country", intoxicated by his secret, the art of snail painting, in which snails that he keeps for the purpose trace their ephemeral slime-trails at night on a black cloth.

The sense of the strange, the mysterious, the mysteriously wonderful is even more awe-inspiring in Nature itself, whether in the cathedral splendour of the equatorial forest, with its "sense of never-ending mystery vast as time / That swallows man" ('Forest Path, Nightfall'), or in the river's unfathomable 'Deep Pool', with its symbolic resonances: "Agony, horror, hate, and fear, / Not reached by measurement, are there." The men who are drawn by the lure of the Essequibo hinterland are like the "cloud of velvet, shimmering moths" that "rise marvellously from the sun-touched bank" to "fly [suicidally] in thousands to the far shore" ('The River-Crossing Moths'). McDonald has his place beside other distinguished writers, like Wilson Harris and Mark McWatt, who have imaginatively explored the Guyanese interior.

Between Silence and Silence brings us a few Georgetown characters, like MacArthur ('MacArthur's Life'), Sing-Song, who worked for forty years as barman at the Parkview Club ('Sing-Song's Place'), and the man who spent a lifetime standing in Main Street blessing the world ('Canticle of the Main Street Madman'). An elegiac quality adds poignancy to these portraits, the characters being now in the twilight of their lives. This elegiac quality is continued in the later poems, in the pieces which speak of the poet's awareness of his own ageing. And yet the sobering awareness of mortality which deepens McDonald's verse is irradiated by his celebration of life, his gratitude for happy days and for earth's bounty of joy. Although 'Shadows Will Hide the Sun', he invokes light on his son at his baptism: "In the dark world / bathe him in light." He remembers his mother remembering "her swift horse", "the fine horse in his gleaming trap", with "the wind blowing in her red, wild hair" ('Beaucaillou'). Ultimately, "Friend, it is past the time when tears matter: / between silence and silence, there should be only praise" ('Between Silence And Silence There Should Be Only Praise'). He considers himself privileged to be able to "write this absurdly happy verse / to tell what it was like once forever" ('What It Was Like Once Forever').

Ian Archie McDonald, eldest of six siblings, was born at St Augustine, Trinidad on April 18th, 1933. His father, born in St Kitts to Antiguan parents, was a lecturer at the Imperial College of Tropical Agriculture at St Augustine, and later Director of Agricultural Holdings at the firm of Gordon Grant. His mother was a Trinidadian of French ancestry.

As a student at Queen's Royal College in Port of Spain, McDonald began writing poetry in the sixth form, under the influence of an Englishman, John Hodge, "who was one of those incredibly inspiring teachers [who] gave ... a group of about five of us this impetus to write". McDonald remembers the impact of Gerard Manley Hopkins' 'The Windhover' as taught by Hodge. There was also the example of his schoolmate V. S. Naipaul, his senior by a year, whom he remembers as being, even from then, "a great figure and considered ... a great eccentric as well". On leaving Queen's Royal College, he entered Cambridge University in 1951 to read for an honours degree in history. He captained the Cambridge lawn tennis team in 1955 and played for and captained the West Indies Davis Cup team at various times between 1953 and the mid-1960s.

Graduating from Cambridge in 1955, he took a job as Secretary to the Bookers Group Committee in what was then British Guiana. He has lived in Guyana ever since. He eventually became Director of Marketing and Administration for the Guyana Sugar Corporation, and later CEO of the Sugar Association of the Caribbean. He did a regular radio commentary, on public affairs, from the late 1970s until the mid-1980s. Since the inception of the *Stabroek News* in 1986, he has contributed a weekly column on a wide range of topics, from politics to ethics to culture to literature and cricket – and has never missed a week. He also served as Editorial Assistant to the West Indian Commission, for which he wrote *Bedrock of a Nation: Cultural Foundations of West Indian Integration* (1992). He assisted in producing the Commission's 1992 report, *Time for Action*.

When McDonald went to live in Guyana in the mid-1950s, there was growing excitement in West Indian literary circles about the new flowering of West Indian literature. The favourable climate owed something to the encouragement and opportunity offered to young writers by the little magazines *Bim* and *Kyk-over-al*, as well as to the weekly BBC programme 'Caribbean Voices'. Not only did McDonald contribute poems regularly to *Bim*, less regularly to *Kyk-over-al* and 'Caribbean Voices', and later to *The Caribbean Writer*, but he also wrote prose fiction and drama. 'Kaiser', an extract from an unpublished novel, appeared in *Kyk* in 1958. The novel, *The Humming-Bird Tree* (1969), was a distinguished contribution to the West Indian novel of childhood. Awarded the Royal Society of Literature Prize, it was made into a film for television, and broadcast, by the BBC, in 1992. His one-act play *The Tramping Man*, first staged in 1969, was published in *A Time and a Season: 8 Caribbean Plays* (ed. Errol Hill, 1976). He edited *AJS at 70* (1984) and has been joint editor of *The Heinemann Book of Caribbean Poetry* (1992), A. J. Seymour's *Collected Poems, 1937-1989* (2000) and *Poems by Martin Carter* (2006). With Seymour, its founder-editor, he helped revive *Kyk-over-al* in 1984. After Seymour's death in 1989, he continued to edit the magazine, and then did so jointly from 1996 until 2000.

McDonald is a Fellow of the Royal Society of Literature. In 1986 he was awarded the Guyana national honour, the Golden Arrow of Achievement. The University of the West Indies conferred on him the honorary degree of Doctor of Letters in 1997.

Dedication

For Mary and my sons Keith, Jamie and Darren
And in remembrance of my parents
John Archie and Thelma McDonald

I wish to express my thanks to Harry Chambers of
Peterloo Poets and Jeremy Poynting of Peepal
Tree Press for their encouragement and for
first publishing most of these poems.

Poems, 1950s and 1960s

Temple Bullock

Strong bullock tugs a corn-laden cart up the dirt hill,
Saliva drips down the slippery black of cut lips,
Falls into the dust at the end of long elastic threads
    of cowspit,
Bright glue in threads like spider silks hung from trees
    some mornings.
Clumsy testicles sway, hitting big legs as he treads on.
The driver beats him methodically without any anger
And the bullock moves not one beaten muscle:
The flies are not disturbed from his mouth.
On the hill stands an Indian temple with white clay walls;
On the walls are painted blue herons and peacock fans,
Strange men in colour-beaded high hats –
On their faces different grimaces of pure emotion,
Cruelty and delicate love.
High white dome of the temple stands strong on the sky,
Good white stone reflecting stars like a pool of water.
Pots of corn stand under the walls.
Drums beat in the bright courtyard.
The soft peculiar wail searching for sadness
Of the religious chant of old Indians
Sweetens the gold air on the hill.
Today is celebrated, you see, the prophet Hossein,
Lover of men and all oxen.

Rumshop Girl

Walked the burnt red roads, looping the green hills
Like red ropes around nine green tons of cane.
Thirsty hours on the road under the honey sun.
Came up to a rumshop on the bright-stoned way.
Ordered hard yellow cheese, thick slices of earth
    brown bread,
Four tall beers dewed with cool keeping.
Life was good. Kicked my boots off under the counter.
It was a joy when the big girl came
With dancing step, full of sweet eyes,
Black face full of dark shining, breast stuffing her blouse.
It was marvellous how she leaned them on the counter
Like fat young pullets, how her thighs bounced.
She clapped down the plate with a sideways look
And poured the cold beers for me with a lazy smile.
While I gulped the beer, cold as creeks,
She stood arms akimbo, making her dark sweet-eyes.
Good to be hungry and eat that cheese, that soft bread.
Good to be thirsty and drink the cold-dewed beer in a gulp.
Good to be a man and see the girl, arms akimbo, make her
    eyes sweet for me.
The sun floods the red road outside;
Smell of warmed flowers, song of corn-birds, dream
    in the air.
What joy to live! Far, far away is death.
Suddenly the girl laughs, I laugh also, we do not speak.

Bright Cockerel

I find a fowl will eat flesh as well as grain and blades of grass.
Here is a bright cockerel picking the bones of a frog under the
    lemon tree.
The bird is finely plumaged, at his tail a cascade of white
    and purple
And at his back a ruff of small red and golden feathers.
Now, bright cockerel, proud bright fowl, red-combed lion,
How could you pick with your white splendid beak
This poor small frog green and delicate as a lily leaf?
How employ the sharp curved sword of your armed and
    golden head
Upon little green frogissimo meek and jewel-bright?
Why peck, bright cockerel, the life out of this little
    mud lover?
Why sully the rich bracelets of your feathers
With blood from out this fish-pawed lesser emerald breed?
Unless the stink of frog bones smelling in the sun
Appeals to you, great bright cockerel of death.

Mais of Jamaica

His own life died but he has not truly died.
There, man! Look, look at him, the writing man,
Muscles of Jamaica's hills carved in his face,
His skin coloured above the blood in brown drought sun,
His hands strong like a carpenter's, his eyes strong,
His work strong, his theme the terrific future of the poor,
Commonplace and powerful as the sea's green weight.
Do not forget him in your ordinary days.
See his paintings there gaunt as starved oxen –
He put his hand to them in no search for praise.
His own life died but he has not truly died.
Man, you have seen a great tree put to the flame
How it roars up red above the land
And nothing will stop the red and fiery tree
Until the red flames eat the tree-heart out,
And then it dies, the good fire dies
But no dying can put the glory out.
So! Touch his life, your heart burns like a fire-tree.

Decorated for a Kiss

I come to her house for love with a basket of red petals.
Man-friend tell me what a fool to go to the girl:
Come, man, come fish shark, strong white shark,
At midnight, come fish, golden snapper along the warm
    black rocks.
But I decide my mind and come to her for love.
Her dress is patterned with blue dragonflies.

4

She has put a red bead in each ear.
Green lizards run in her eyes.
Her body has the scent of sun-dried khus-khus grass –
The sweet fibres she has put between the linen
    since midday.
She has washed her mouth with milk,
She has rubbed her lips with bay leaves,
Made her limbs clean with water from a green calabash.
Now she offers me a few plums and palm-wine from a gourd
    of scarlet leather.

Young Harpooner

At low tide the jetty stands with socks of moss on its
    caterpillar feet.
He lies on his belly on the warm and slippery planks
    of wood,
Fishes for eels and peacock fish with cork and hook and
    shrimp-bait.
Ah! the smell of salt and tar in the wood and the feel of
    the green waves pulling the cord.
Suddenly! gliding bat fish, black stingray, passes at three
    yards' distance –
A small one only but enough to set the boy's heart mad
    with courage for the open sea,
For standing like the one-legged seaman in his boot shining
    harpoon in young hand,
With landless eyes on the waves coming like giant redfish
    as the sun flames at the horizon.
His soul fills with the silence and the fierceness of the sea.

Lonely Near Educated Water

Here evening spends its hundred hours –
Drinking red water from white-jellied coconuts
Sharpening itself on blue rock
Buying from the merchant with golden cloths
Climbing green Japon hill
Jubilant in the red heavens
Like a paradise of fair-boys
Visiting the moon for bundles of silver sticks
Chasing the wild black pigs in the black bush.
Wrecks of gold and scarlet barques float
In the immense India of the sky.
I am seated in the nut grass by this green pond
Quiet amidst the Israelic chirring of brown grasshoppers.
I have been so for one hot, still evening hour
At watch on the goldfish burning in the water,
Slender unquenchable ingots in this gentle green element.
Round the pond is a mosaic of ordinary bright stones.
Patterns of flowers and lions create themselves in the mosaic.
A lizard green as grass slips away in the amber light.
I am lonely near educated water.
I have nothing better to do than suck quite dry
A yellow hairy mango seed old as yesterday
Long after it has lost its last, lost flavours.

The Legend of Mangamuch and La Cour Harpe

Our epics begin to form.
I know the great stick-fight is one: the stone pictures have
    been carved of it.
It was near Rio Claro, between the champions of
    the batoniers,
The giant Mangamuch, hard bitter La Cour Harpe, the
    two fighters.

The Negres jardens with their jointed tambour bamboos,
    goat-skinned, many-coloured,
Beat the news of a major bataille bois days and days ahead,
    honoured to be proclaimers.
Men came from seventy villages barefoot or in donkey carts
And the women carrying melons and coconuts to sell
    in the hot afternoon.
And even three sunburnt Englishmen in white drill and
    brown cork hats came!

When the last goat-skin drum faded in silence
All was very quiet around the fighting pit and the sun
    very hot there on the charred ground.
Small boys in the surrounding plum and calabash trees
    watched with flaming eyes;
These men in khaki shorts and belts of dogs' teeth were the
    strongest champions of their blood.

The wary beginning, the skilful work of the stick-stick, sweet
    to the eyes of the old men.
Then the heavier direct blows with their weight of knotty
    black muscles.
They fought all morning with hard watchful eyes

And all afternoon the hard poui sung wapp, wapp, a tinge of
    iron in the wood.
They rested for one hour when night was coming like a great
    black pig.
All the colours of the day came back to burn and praise
    them in the sky.
Then the women bathed their flesh with cool water and gave
    them to drink and corn cakes to eat.
Then followers set up the flambeaux on iron drums in
    the circle
And they fought again by orange flames in the rich,
    furious pit.
The silence of a thousand silent men around the hard
    singing wapp, wapp of the poui sticks.
Three stars flashed with silver tails above in the black night,
    good sign of God's interest.

Mangamuch had five broken fingers and all his fingernails
    were torn off.
La Cour Harpe had deep injuries in his belly and his face
    burnt with the sweat in the poui cuts.
But both had their eyes still to judge and hit and parry well,
So they fought, calm-eyed. Man thought they would
    fight forever
And, indeed, as men will tell you, they fought for longer
    than forever.
Then Mangamuch with the giant's strength in the hot
    second afternoon
Swung his red poui for the thousandth time and La Cour
    Harpe had only bitter weakness.
The blow, swung from great shining arms, burst six of all
    his white ribs.

A shout more of general glory than of single pride for
    either man
Sprung around the fighters. Two small boys fell off a
    calabash tree in excitement!
Pouches of jumby beads and pennies were cast in the
    scarred pit. They sang of it after,
With the sweet-harsh songs, songs of the stick-men for
    Mangamuch and La Cour Harpe.
O! The strong kalindas shouted by the red-sleeved
    jacket-men,
"Je t'aime, Mangamuch, je t'aime, triste Harpe, je vous
    aime, grands noirs hommes."
From the moon of a humming-bird's wing to the moon of a
    rich plum
The legend springs in the song, finds roots as tough as the
    nut grass.

Greeneyes

By the green pool where the milk-bit cascadura is caught
    at morning
I meet my girl whose breasts have the scent of the
    sun-dried khus-khus grass.
I have nothing, greeneyes, better to say to you than this:
for me you are the last dimension in the touch of sense –
berry leaf, cocoa flower along its branch, white lilies
    near Easter River,
in them intricate as length and depth and colour,
as time they last, you are the binder of their form.

All my love you have brought them to the fullness of a
    season's rains
and now the balata tree has leaf falling to the
    stream-ferns
near this green and cascadura-haunted pool;
it is you who are its maker, meaner, who strips the tree
    to its diamond heart.
Come, greeneyes, feel the water like cold bracelets
    round your thighs.

Walking on Lily Leaves

The brown boys have a game they play: it is a rare
    philosophical game.
In the streams under the old trees when they slow to
    sluggish ponds,
Where stick-bodied dragonflies with red paper wings are
    adroit in skips on the surface,
Water lilies grow from the stones and their green leaves
    float on the water.
Fully grown the leaves are almost tough enough to stand in
    but not quite.
So each boy will jump softly from the bank full of ferns
    to one leaf, a second
Before it sinks jump to another leaf as deftly as tallymen
    and the game ends at the end of water lilies.
The floating leaves are of course crushed into the sluggish
    water and the lily flowers go too.
I played that game. I hear still the laughter on the
    lady-slippered bank.
Death in the long river of lilies invades my heart,
    grown old, grown iron.

Jaffo the Calypsonian

Jaffo was a great Calypsonian, fire ate up his soul to sing
    and play calypso iron music.
And when he was small he made many-coloured ping-pong
    drums and searched them for the island music,
Drums of beaten oil-barrel iron daubed in triangles, with
    stolen paint from a harbour warehouse.
Now he seized the sorrow and the bawdy farce in metal-harsh
    beat and his own thick voice.
He was not famous in the tents; he went there once and not a
    stone clapped and he was afraid of respectable eyes,
The white-suited or gay-shirted lines of business men or
    tourists muffled his deep urge.
But he went back to the Indian tailor's shop and sung well
    and to the Chinese and sweepstake shop and sung well,
Unsponsored calypsos, and in the scrap lots near the Dry
    River lit by one pitch-oil lamp or two
He would pound his ping-pong and sing his hoarse voice out
    for ragged still-eyed men.
But in the rumshop he was best, drinking the heavy sweet
    molasses rum he was better than any calypso man,
In front of the rows of dark red bottles, in the cane-scented
    rooms his clogged throat rang and rang with staccato chant.
Drunk then, he was best, easier in pain from the cancer in
    his throat, but holding the memory of it.
On the rough floors of rumshops, strewn with bottle-tops
    and silver-headed corks and broken green bottle-glass
He was released from pain into remembered pain, his thick
    voice rose and grated in brassy fear and fierce joke.
His voice beat with bitterness and fun, as if he told of old
    things, hurt ancestral pride and great slave-humour –

He would get a rum if he sung well so perhaps there was
    that of it too –
He was always the best, though, he was the best: the ragged
    men said so, and the old men.
One month before he died his voice thickened to a hard
    final silence;
The look of unsung calypsos stared in his eyes, a terrible
    thing to watch in the rat-trap rumshops.
When he could not stand with pain he was taken in the
    public ward of the Colonial Hospital.
Rafeeq, the Indian man who in Marine Square watches
    the birds all day for his God, was there also.
Later he told about Jaffo in a long mad chant to the
    rumshop men; they laughed at the story.
Until the end Jaffo stole spoons from the harried nurses
    to beat rhythm on his iron bedposts.

Pineapple Woman

Selling pineapple is she art
Sad old woman pushing cart

Near Dutch Stabroek every day
You can find she minding tray

Full of sunripe 'Quibo pine
"Come an' buy me God-ripen pine!"

When the sun is hot and gold
Old woman get she pineapple sold

Rich lady come with palmolive skin
Then the bargaining fun begin

Rich woman probably good at heart
But she got to bargain to play the part

So while silver shilling busting she purse
She letting fly with less pence than curse

And old woman with she age and pine
Have to cut the price down fine

So she squatting down beside she tray
Twelve hard hours by the end of she day

Pineapple ripe smelling sweet of sun
Turning she belly by the time day done

Dollar fifty profit from the fat gold pine
If a day make so much she doing fine

And go down Stabroek in Maytime rain
Look for that old pine woman again

She old grey dress busting away
Rotting and fade in the rains of May

But she under the branch of a samaan tree
Still working out she destiny

Selling pines from 'Quibo fat and gold
Until the heart inside she chest get cold

Forty years by Stabroek rain and shine
Sad old woman selling pine

And when she dead by a 'Quibo charcoal pit
Nobody bother or care one shit

She was buying pine to sell in the morning
But she never reach to sell that morning

Stabroek look the same old way
In suns of March or rains of May.

Mystic at the Nightclub Miramar

He sits by the rum-sweet bar: an Indian mystic.
His eyes are lightless, his cheek-bones stretch the
    dry skin,
His white moustaches are stained yellow up at the roots
From eating curry-cakes or smoking bamboo leaf tobacco.
Every Wednesday he comes to sit, watching the dancers,
Watching with white still eyes the men drinking rum,
The sweaty dance band, trombonist in a red sweater,
Golden Madeline the whore and Jackman full of calypso.
He has a bag of shells and when he goes he leaves one on
    the bar.
Then on Thursday morning he walks five miles from
    his village
To Caroni river where he spits into the brown water
And walks back: penance for a whole world's
    crazed direction.

The Stick-Fighters

Lives form around facts and the greatest lives around the
  greatest facts –
So the old men speak of the bataille bois; their greatest fact.
Where are La Cour Harpe and Gros Adams, Tiepin, and
  Chinee Patrick, the great stick-fighters,
Laptong, Blood, and Muscovi, the old heroes of Cobeau Town?
They wielded the yard-long poui sticks, polished, balanced
  in a fine way,
Centred with charms, snake-teeth or bones from the
  Belmont graveyard.
The fine ritual is lost of the precise harsh art of it.
They say Placide could with his quick wrist beat away any
  stone flung at his body.
Oh fine art! Fierce game for only the calm-eyed!
On Carnival day, Jour Ouvert: the colour of it, the
  jacket-men in scarlet sleeves
And their big-hipped women carrying rum and roasted
  breadfruit and cassava cakes.
The fighter's challenge then: "Zingay Talala mettex la main
  asu moi!"
And the tough-skinned batoniers urged by the stick-cry
  "Quaray! Quaray!" Proud men.
And after: the stick songs, sweet kalindas, beat on bamboo
  drums stretched with many-coloured goat-skin,
Song throbbing in the red throats of the fight-contented.
Ha! Great days then, hard boys, hard blows, say old men.
Of the blood pits of Sangre Grande can be told endless
  strong tales
But in the green hills now only the whine of hill-women
  cutting grasses.

The Four Knives of Freeman, the Cane-Cutter

The four knives of Freeman, the cane-cutter, are famous
    in his village.
Man call him Knife-man and praise the marvellous handles
    and cold, sharp blades.
One knife is bone-handled and that red-veined bone was the
    stamping foot of a black mare once,
Pared and shaped and polished with chisel and rough
    steel file.
That knife he has cut a man with who hurt his wife near the
    water-rock one night.
The handle of his second famous knife is of hard lime wood
    seasoned yellow with vinegar.
Like a fat stick of old ivory it is and round it fastened
    three thin bands of green leather.
It handles easily, the exquisite balance of it lies deep
    in his fingers.
This is his throwing knife: with it he can split a dog's
    wagging tail twenty feet away.
His third knife is rose-coloured and has small dragons
    carved in that blood-stone handle.
Men admire the golden pebbles of wood laid in the dragons'
    eye-sockets with infinite, infinite artistry
And they admire the curved blade of it, thin as a leaf and
    glazed with silver.
This is the most precious of his famous knives. A collector
    offered for it one hundred dollars
But Freeman, the cane-cutter, will not sell: he keeps it
    at his belt
Beautiful to see in its white-skinned sheath of
    fringed leather.

And sometimes villagers watch him peel fruit with it or
    carve boys' whistles and crucifixes for the Church.
But his fourth knife is different: there gathers in it from a
    long-remembered history a separate value.
From generation to generation the faith of men has entered
    into the long blade and the shell handle.
It is used for only one work; it can have no other; it is a
    consecrated knife.
The knife hangs above his bed at night like a holy cross,
    holy indeed to him.
For when the slaves were freed an old man took it from the
    saddle-sheath of his overseer and ran to the saving hills:
In his mind the story of its special use began. Dying, he
    gave it to a son
And from this son the famous knife has come through
    generations to Freeman, still the cane-cutter.

What European craftsman toiled to make the knife, its blade
    rich and edged to cut-bone sharpness
Its palm-worn handle a treasury of sea colours? Now a
    symbol for a black man,
An ancient gesture grown large to hold the meaning of
    man's humility and a slave's defiance
For Freeman uses his fourth famous knife only in the
    fields, uses it to cut the emerald ancestral cane.

Indian Love Statement

Tassim loves her like an idiot, makes himself a saga boy,
Puts green cedar leaves to scent his clothes, sweetens his
    hair with bay rum.
He makes sweet eyes at her all day and praises her
    green eyes.
He does nothing practical, his only gift is sentiment.
I, on the other hand, am determined to make less brittle
    love to her.
Though I am, as I will be, overall gentle, I bring her
    not a little pride and confidence.
Also I bring her faults: she knows the smell of my sweaty
    armpits if I work hard.
I do not hide it: cane-field sweat is good water.
Nor do I hide some roughness in my manners, being unused
    to Tassim and his like.
Yet I bring her also gifts and assurances of love, a basket
    of oranges,
A parasol of rough blue cotton stemmed and ribbed
    with bamboo,
Beads, candied shaddocks, rings, everything I bring her
    in shrewd love.

The Seine-Pullers

On the sand under the loose-leaved tree I watch the
    seine-pullers: for me a romance.
There is no romance for the toilsmen as for them it is
    a plain work for eating.
They pull the seine in long powerful tugs, pull the seine,
In long perpetual tugs they pull the seine and pull
    the seine,
Twenty men on the salt ropes to their knees in strong water
In trousers of sailcloth and handkerchief hats and
    necklaces of seabone.
Their women ready with baskets for the fish sit at the back
    of the beach with their children.
Sharks and cutlass fish which are bright and sharp begin to
    beat in the closing urn of water,
The tugs quicken and the corks on the black net toss closer
    in the broken green waves.
The men get the smooth clubs ready; the small boys smile
    brilliantly with excitement –
They, like myself, watch for the terrible shining fish,
    expect the sea to unsheathe wonderful swords –
The men and women hope for a profitable catch bringing
    many silver pence.
I in the end see a flail from the grave sea beat silver rainbows
    up and in its leap with colours
The mackerel shines in the morning air a long time after
    its protest at the shallowness.
There is a murmur then for that fish means thirty shillings
    in the market.

Statement to God

Things of the world, things of my flesh, facets of all
    sensual being:
Diamonds in the water-grass, clear stars above Mount
    Saint Benedict,
Wood shone by the great sea, the beauty in birds,
Induce me towards God, or at least make me love what they
    seem to mean.
This morning I saw a red locust on the fruit of a carob tree,
Its flare of scarlet made me love the maker of such
    scarlet art.
But I want no sweet signs or tremendous signs of the
    unsensed original:
Only to find a bare love come by a plain way,
And take such love to be eternal habit, ornamentless, mild,
Direct as a peasant's drinking cup of clay,
A woman's hand that daily feeds a child.

Georgetown Children

Under the soursop silver-leaf tree
The High School children play skip-and-free

Sun burning down like a fire ball
Watch the children before school call

Laugh in their gay time, laughter rich
Jump the jack, bring marble pitch

Black child, yellow child, brown child, white
They all the same if you looking right

Pass by any schoolyard in Georgetown at all
And watch the children before school call

Under the soursop silver-leaf tree
The High School children play skip-and-free.

The biggest thing in life could be
Watching the children play skip-and-free.

Hispaniola

Hispaniola is an old white aristocrat
The demon of his life, a black cat

Which he killed as a schoolboy long ago
With a golden arrow from a rosewood bow.

Now it combs his beard with its silver claws
It pads on his heart with printless paws

It scratches his belly with undrawn scar
This cat-ghost relentless, black avatar.

An amethyst glows in vain, in vain
From the iron top of his daggered cane

He cuts and stabs at elusive it
But the cat's a cat that never'll be hit.

History-long Hispaniola asked the Why
With dust in his throat, red-flecked his eye:

The scaffolding of his mind eased down
And soon he lived only in feline town

Where a black cat stood at each street turning
And each street lamp was a cat's eye burning.

Hispaniola old waned to final age
His teeth still ivories of crystal rage

But last night over his ebony incense bowl
Black fur closed on Hispaniola's soul.

And tomorrow night they'll find in his heart I know
A cat's claw shot from a rosewood bow.

Railwaymen

The Railway shines like swords through Tunapuna.
Now, stand by the morning market near the bright tracks –
The early sky full of red fruit:
For sale, slain agoutis with golden eyes –
And watch the black trains trample the bright swords:
Storm-arsed, stallion powerful, black iron fire-guts:
Railwaymen are heroes, man!

Railwaymen discover the way of life, like poets.
They feed the train's fire and roaring life with jewels
    of coal,
They throw it in with heavy hot iron shovels
And the new flames warm and redden their hard cheeks,
Especially hard cheeks, railwayman's cheeks, tough like
    black leather.

And the poet might seem a softer man but he shovels too
And flames flush out the black jewels from his iron shovel
Make his stern cheeks lined as old black leather folded
    for one life,
Clean hard the slag-black jewels into pure diamond.

Pelting Bees

By July the bees have built in the samaans:
There are honey-hives in the notches of those burly
    trees there.
Today is Sunday. I go out and pelt them with white stones;
And duck quick under the river-bank, my feet in the
    cold water on the white stones.
How they get up in golden arms then and make a noise
    like breezes!
I hide and watch and again throw white stones with the
    strength of my arm!
Nectar-sweet streams from the rich red honeycombs,
The golden bees blaze with fury in the sun.
I laugh and laugh, pelting white stones from the safety
    of Easter River.

Yusman Ali, Charcoal Seller

Some men have lives of sweet and seamless gold,
No dent of dark or harshness mars those men,
Not Yusman Ali though, not that old charcoal man
Whose heart I think has learned to break a hundred times
    a day:
He rides his cart of embered wood in long agony.

He grew rice and golden apples years ago.
He made an ordinary living by the long mud shore,
Laughed and drank like any other man and planned his four
    sons' glory.
His young eyes watched the white herons rise like flags
And the sun brightening on the morning water in his fields.
His life fell and broke like a brown jug on a stone.
In middle age his four sons drowned in one boat up a
    pleasant river.
The wife's heart cracked and Yusman Ali was alone,
    alone, alone.
Madness howled in his head. His green fields died.

He burns the wild wood in his barren yard alone,
Sells the charcoal on the villaged coast and feasts on stars.
Thinness makes a thousand bones around his scorched heart.
His moon-scarred skin is sick with boils and warts,
His grey beard stinks with goat-shit, sweat and coal.
Fire and heated dust have rawed his eyes to redness:
The eyes hit like iron bullets in my guts.
No kindness in him: the long whip smashes on the donkey
    like an iron.
The black and brittle coal has clogged his chest with dirt,
The black fragrance of the coal is killing him.

He is useful still. I shake with pain to see him pass.
He has not lost his hating yet, there's that sweet thing
    to say,
He farts at the beauty of the rain-dipped moon.
The smooth men in their livery of success
He curses in his killing heart
And yearns for thorns to tear their ease.
His spit blazes in the sun. An emperor's bracelet shines.

Poem on a Black Stone

I walked in a bright river – cool, silver walking.
In the shallows I saw a black stone shining:
Black as the sapodilla seed shining in its flesh,
Charred in the fire of old moons,
Buried in green mountains, covered by worlds of earth,
Tumbled in huge downfalls of cold and sharpened ice,
Washed clean, smooth, in churns of golden ore.
So it was fashioned precisely for my fingers,
Balanced and shone, fruit of the turning suns.

It is suited for the young girl who is my lover,
Black scarab from the silver river for her breast,
Brown girl, so young, no pain yet come to her.
Gently she sleeps now, but I am sleepless in her arms.
The sheets sweat beneath my heavy body.
She holds the black stone near her unknowing heart.
Her fingers touch it in her quiet sleep;
She has greatly treasured this simple gift from me.
Despair withers my old and blazing heart.
I get up on one elbow to watch her carefully.
She is so young, her beauty is not marked,

Youth breathes with grace in every line of her,
She has thrown her dark limbs like a child.
Suddenly I dread cold death's coming:
Dry bone blowing in the wind,
Pulp of eye unseeing, not anymore flesh curving on the bone.

Morning will come.
I will take the black stone from my love.
I will smile at her and explain nothing.
I will carry the black stone up the mountain path,
Walk through the green ferns dewed by night,
The early sun rising, warming the roots of the trees.
I will throw the black stone in the cold and silver river,
Secret it will lie a thousand centuries more.

On an Evening Turned to Rain

Visiting the seaman's ward a hot afternoon
I discovered the old man dying, dying fast,
The rattle in him, the black crow flying near.
The walls dewed grey, the hard beds crowded close,
The smell of deaths, the old routine of cure,
Of alcohol, rough sheets cleaned a thousand times, urine
    splashed like holy water.

No one saw the dying of the old man –
All, all encased in dreams of life –
Until a nurse came with some tenderness
(I well remember her, she hard and tall as a post)
And took his hand, with some tenderness I say,
Hand frail as ash waiting for wind to blow.
And she held his hand until the black crow settled firm.

I wandered near, death's mystery a lure,
And heard the low words almost break his teeth:
"I live a good life, and now I dead!"
To write it straight as bone is not to say it well.
Slimed by black belly juices the tongue fell out of him:
The nurse stood up and cleaned his vomit up.
I knew him well, a strong man in his day.
The black crow cawed, rattling a joyful wing
And so the old man died, leaving his words to me.

There is a bureaucracy for moving people on: they
    buried him quick
That evening, turned to rain.
Your funeral cart, my reader, will be more glorious
    than his:
Think now of your heaped flowers, not for him!
No man shall go naked to his cavern-rest:
A grey robe sheeted him, rough as cattle tongue,
A lead medallion twined his neck for long identity.
(So, old counterfeit Pharaoh! They left you that last
    treasure!)
When the world overturns, they say, God will know his bones.
He had a pauper's grave, black hole glistening in the earth.
Narrow moats with lilies red and sweet as flesh,
And palms wave above in melancholy green.
In rainy times the trenches swamp the burial places of
    the poor;
The rich man's bones keep dry on higher ground.
He had his retinue like any other man:
The grave-diggers, brawny-young and laughing,
And the lantern-carrier, uncle of a thousand deaths,
And myself, watchman at a distance, not near enough for
    love or work.

An old moon coming up, a cold wind blowing,
The rain drifting in, bringing the smell of the sea.
No one claimed him, no sons came.

His words pursued me as I followed him.
"I live a good life, and now I dead!"
I puzzle at the old man's meaning.
He was so certain when he spoke,
He had an idea in his mind I'm sure,
He had to say his chosen words out clear,
They almost broke his teeth to say.
Silence was not good enough for him:
The breath inside him screeched like a sharpened bone.
Was it defiance that he spoke?
Proud of living well in full enjoyment,
Women fucked and fondled, wine drunk down,
Every pleasure tasted in his young and middling life,
And now he thought of that and spat a curse at death?
Could that be it? Or was it black agony of loss?
Of loss and bitter disillusion, his words an agony:
"I live a good life, and now I dead!"
So much of sacrifice offered up, no justice in return,
Was that the thought that struggled to be said:
Each man who dies, he dies in desperation,
Like a stray cat strangling in a ditch?
Or was it fierce eternal faith,
An echo of the saint's calm prayer:
Let nothing disturb thee
Let nothing affright thee
All passeth away.
God alone will stay?

The ashes of the old man's words I taste:
I think of Gandhi in his hungering quest,
Of Hitler in his iron hate,
Of emperors polishing bright swords of war,
Of poets practising their songs of love,
Beggarman, I think of you.
The dark evening turns to heavier rain.
My thoughts' confusion troubles me.
All, all are pity's children
All will go out like flame.
The water cleans the old man in his grave forever.

State of the Nation

Affairs in the young Republic do not go well.
Problems weigh like stones on every man.
In everyone's heart there is growing doubt.
The most placid have begun to grumble:
The playing children notice the unusual scowls.
In the rumshops there is moody silence, with bursts
    of anger,
And the churches are filled with arid sermons.
The nation seems to trudge a weary road:
On all sides ardour is withdrawn.

It is not that progress is not made.
No, the burnished buildings grow,
Machinery hums in the new factories,
Bush is cleared and new crops are extended.
Men are urged to be prouder and are probably so;
Beards sprout fearlessly, non-colonial clothes sell in
    all the shops.

Great advances are made in education and medical care.
Our foreign embassies every day report fresh
    diplomatic initiatives.
New dances are discovered for the new culture.

The people are a flame, not easily put out,
Unless you raze wide swathes around their rights.
What has happened? why are knives pulled in the street?
There is not much time, that is generally recognised.

Drunk

There is a young man, always drunk,
Nobody has respect for him in this town,
He has let down his respectable parents.
I say he is young, but now he is not so young:
Grey threads of hair sparkle in his beard.

Ever since, he was badly behaved, this man,
From young days he was always getting drunk:
He would go to the cricket and shout with joy,
He would direct bustling traffic in the middle of Water Street,
Hot noondays would find him feeding birds in the Gardens.
He would go to parties in mad clothes, in ridiculous hats,
Spill drinks, swing pretty girls squealing in the air,
He could never at all be serious in any work.
He entered the Civil Service, the first day he was drunk:
He engaged his superiors in poetic argument.
He would draw bright cartoons on the important files
And say in a loud voice: "This is cock, man, this is
    truly cock!"
He did not last long, lacking the necessary application.

He was idle mostly, rum-soaked in beer pavilions.
Once he went on the savannahs, burning, swept by wind,
He came back with his beard and a little gold,
His pockets full of jaguar blood,
Green locusts tangled in his hair,
Stars of coldness on his tongue.
He spent the gold feting up his friends, and
    a few prostitutes,
Strangely mixed, but the fete was good, full of joy,
Everybody in town talked about him, laughed scornfully.

He is getting older now, his vigour more subdued:
People hurry past this drunk man, showing sour faces.
He came to my house Sunday, frailer than I remember,
He asked for bread to eat, and a cup of cool water.
All he wanted – bread, a cup of water, and a little talk:
Talk of his roaring times, the heroes at the cricket matches,
The clashing games of dominoes, the brawling bars of
    Tiger Bay,
The roistering, the love affairs, the carnivals of rum.
But once, before he ended, he told a different tale:
His eye looked serious in my eye, burning to convince,
From boyhood days he loved wild birds:
In books he wrote their colours down,
Their ways of flight, their gleaming wings,
He had them all in memory,
Every bird in this wide land,
He told me how he followed them,
Not drunken then in his wild chase:
Not drunken then in that devotion.

My drunken visitor has gone,
His begging bowl is full with bread.

I sit in silence in my home,
Sober in this quiet town,
The peace of Sunday settles down,
He walks away, his back hunched up,
The grey hairs sparkle in his beard,
The sunset on him burns and glows.
I see him through the mist of years:
He goes to chase the gold-winged hawks,
His eyes ablaze for humming-birds.

The spurwings circle around his head,
The corn-birds land upon his arm,
And drunken in their sun-filled games,
The river-swallows dance for him.

The Weather in Shanty Town

The poets sing, the sweet words gleam like shining laces:
"When the sun harnesses the earth like a goldsmith,
Praise the rain, praise the cold lady rain!
When the black storm throws pelting rain down in spears,
Praise the fire of the sun, praise the gold wand of the sun!
This land is land of big weathers, black and gold;
Storms and fierce heat descend like cruel princes,
Black warlords in their thunder palaces.
Under the new moon sometimes there is peace of weather,
Rain falling like white lilies on the iron streets:
Praise, praise the convenor of the dark winds, the
    bright airs!"

No poets' words for shanty town: the weather kills and
    cankers every day.

The black storm in the morning shakes the tilting huts.
Women stuff the cracked walls full with rags against the
    pour of rain.
Their children play in drowning pools, laughing in the
    sudden mud.
The black rain and the flail of storm is horrible:
The sodden damp stinking, cesspits overflowing,
    dryness nowhere.
The water pearls on black tin walls in sweating dews
    of filth.
The wet air swims like slime in every space and lung.
The rain is piss in shanty town, it brings no grace
    of silver.

Another day the avid sun hammers the hard earth gold.
Flies blacken the silver eyes of dead pigs in the
    dumping grounds.
Dust stuffs the bright air streaming from the sky.
It is hot as ovens, hot as engines, hot as deserts.
The heat simmers, the sun sings in the air,
    torpor everywhere.
The scums of old rain crack like scabs on beggars' sores.
The brass of sunlight poisons shanty town, the hot air
    fumes with shame.
The smell rises in a shimmering fog, a smell of death
    and guts.
Black vultures land with dusty wings to browse on
    heated filth;
The children blaze with joy and race to catch them on the
    carrion grounds.

Men in good clothes do not feel the weather.
Men sweet with food do not fear the weather.
Men in shining cars glide easy through all weather.
Paper-mighty men at desks do not hate the weather.
Men in strong houses do not know the weather of this world.
Such men, such cocooned men, they do not live in
    shanty town.
The weather in their hearts is mild, they have not lived in
    shanty town.
In shanty town the anger hangs like smoke, like fire.
The weather in those hearts is storm, the weather in those
    hearts is hate.

Poems, early to mid-1980s

Nurse Guyadeen and the Preacher

Best nurse in here was Sati Guyadeen
Bright, loving, strict, humorous and clean.
Dealt briskly with every single chore
Yet strove beyond "Accept, endure."
Sati Guyadeen, fresh morning breeze,
Stepping in on edge of dance,
You made a difference in this place.
Who claims even half-perfection?
Hope and bravery in every glance
You nudged life in the right direction.

Big feud broke out once in here:
It livened up the Ward a while.
They brought in Herman Forrester
A pavement-preacher all his life.
He had his pitch in Water Street:
Up and down the pave all day,
"Save your soul: Repent, repent!
The world it end tonight at eight.
Repent, repent! It not too late!"
Every Friday eleven o'clock
He took his stand by Royal Bank:

"Money is the root of all evil,
It eat out your soul like biscuit-weevil!"
And Wednesday by J. P. Santos store
He lectured on Mosaic law.

In here he didn't stop for breath
All day you heard his preacher-mouth:
"Repent your sins before you die!"
If you were God's children, then all right:
He pointed straight up in the sky.
But when he said where sinners go
He pointed dramatically low
Implying that those he saw around
Would taste hell-fire underground.
In all the Ward distress began:
They frighten of this preacher man.
Who with, say, a month to go
Likes to be condemned below?

Nurse Guyadeen, brisk and firm,
Decide herself to handle him.
"People can't have peace in here?
Hush up, or water pour on you!"
(She would have poured a drop or two.)
The big feud start up straight away:
Preacher-man forget to preach,
He have a new thing now to do:
Bad-talking Guyadeen black and blue.
"Parrot-monkey, La Penitence rat,
Guyadeen more ugly than that!"

He spends his hours thinking hard
And looking happy when he could shout
"Someone smell like pit-latrine
It must have to be Nurse Guyadeen!"
And Guyadeen giving as good as got
Lip match lip, hot for hot
And when she think he gets too fas'
She jam an enema up his arse.
The quarrel kept the whole Ward bright:
Who win today was the talk tonight.
For a good ten days they had it out
Row for row, shout for shout,
But I noticed how she took her cue:
He began to weaken, she weakened too.
The last few days it didn't count
His mind wandered North and South
Sweet Jesus walked in Stabroek Market
And honey rained on Zion's Mount.
"Good riddance!" claimed Nurse Guyadeen
When she came to hear he died at noon;
Set straight about her many tasks,
Brought clean sheets, plumped up the pillows.
The empty bed was filled by six,
The new chart written up and fixed.
She made sure the night-lamps all were lit
And then she cried a little bit.

Axed Man

"Bad-bad case of sugar:
They had to cut him down."
The old man sits upright, rigid,
Spine straight against heaped pillows.
He grips the bedclothes on both sides.
Big-torsoed, bull-necked, muscled man
Wears faded-red, short pyjama pants
Just folding over both new bandaged stumps.
No toes, no feet, no shins, no legs
No knees to kneel on any longer
To pray to God for mercy, rest.
Yesterday they "cut him down" again
But still an obscure stink prevails.

Matron knows his story: strong once,
A timber man, big as the trees he killed.
He lived in forests and towered over men,
A rollicking and famous working man:
Ten times won at Mashramani time
Who could chop a great tree down the fastest.
He logged purple-heart and teak and silverballi:
Trees falling give a sense of exultation.
Look at his stumps now!
The axe in the end
Missed horribly.

The Last Classroom of Hubertus Jones

Hubertus Jones was teacher to the bone:
Fifty years in schools in Golden Grove.
His wit unvarying as the texts he taught:
Mark him down five in scale ten to nought.
Term after term infinitely unwound
Plain and strict and dull and sound.
Taught unchanging what he could teach,
The generations soared beyond his reach.
Cord-thin, very neat, and spare
His routines recurring, his rules austere,
He made no money, so he ended here.

People lonely, sick, and old
Have strange dreams in Mercy Ward:
When they "go off" no fuss is made,
They are soothed or chided, then tucked back in.
So Schoolmaster Jones pursued his career,
Taught a full class and set them homework.
Once a week he had Matron fired
For failing to do what he required
And confirmed in writing to Central Board
All that was wrong in Mercy Ward.

What eases the heart should never be grudged:
When anyone departed his last classroom
Hubertus Jones called for paper and pen
And it was seriously brought for him to compose
A concise and lucid term's review
Of conduct, aptitude, and future ambitions
For possible use by the powers that be.
He carefully handed them in on completion

And Matron would promise to deliver them safe.
Meticulous in all he ever did
He kept file copies for easy referral.

When Hubertus Jones departed in turn
I had a look at his filed returns.
Everyone was given precisely his due
But I noticed something shining through:
In the very worst cases of condemnation
He always added a last recommendation:
"Whatever his misdemeanours here on earth
He should be given a chance to prove his worth."

Scrappy little man, Hubertus Jones:
God spare us all, and rest his bones.

Not Here

Somewhere
A bird sings.
Sound of ping-pong balls
Batted to and fro,
Kitchen-clatterings,
A shooing of dogs.
Wind-murmurs
In green trees.
Laughter-spiced talk
Somewhere,
Not here.

Royal Visit

Once Mercy Ward was heaped with flowers.
A serious princess from the British Isles
Asked what more duty she could do
To fill a Sunday morning she had spare.
They really spruced the place up then:
Cleaners scrubbed the floor with non-carbolic soap,
Swept roach wings, mouse shit, all away,
Air freshener used to help the winds of May.
Mercy Ward was clean as heaven.

And everywhere it blazed with flowers.
The Parks Commission sent their gardeners.
Truckloads of greenery and flowers came:
Great, lovely clumps of flaming bougainvillea,
Roses in profusion and Barbados Pride,
Blue plumbago and sweet jump-up-and-kiss,
Vases lent and filled with fragrant plants,
Exotic orchids pale in beds of fern,
Blood-red hibiscus and flowers of the sun.
(Would all their funerals fetch half so much?)

Only old Mangru, not known for being difficult,
Spoiled the great occasion somewhat.
When she stopped and asked him very nicely how he was
He sucked his few teeth quite hard and long:
For all the sour stares from Matron at the back
He simply would not smile or say a single word.
Even worse than that, old-stager Mangru,
When she was three beds further on,
Amidst the healthy dignitaries, all those lovely blooms,
Gave forth the loudest fart you ever, ever heard.

Discharged

They cannot keep you in this place
If you are sure you do not want to stay.
You can discharge yourself at any time:
You have that option, it is your privilege.
Naturally they try to persuade you differently.
Mostly it is possible to ease the patient back
But sometimes a little vigour must be used:
The tough attendants use a slap or two
To make a man see sense, and only for his sake.

But one night, dismal with a rainy moon,
The young man in row 6, bed 22,
Solitary, silent, making no fuss at all,
Broke a hidden drinking glass
And under the covering sheets pulled right up
Cut both his wrists, deeply, surely,
One by one carefully, firmly,
And discharged himself.
They came running in the morning
But not even the tough ones
Could coax him back.

Candle-Light

No beauty
Is here
It is stark.
But one night
Light failed
Over half the town;
The old generator
Took its time to start.
In that instant
Candle-flies in season,
Brightening and fading,
Were hundreds in the room
As if girls
Had flung them
At a wedding.

That once,
Such beauty
In this sad place,
The glimmering
Of candle-flies.

Monster

Black eyes
Without tears.
Terrible seeing a child
That will not cry.
A monster's eyes:
The giant worm of hunger
Swells her belly.
It lies curled there,
It has wound itself upwards
And stares out the sockets
Of her emptied eyes.

The Dwarf Dogs of Montserrat

Jumpy on twin leashes
Panting pink tongues
Gold-speckled eyes
Scarlet-collared
Silver-tagged like gifts
Miniature and manicured:
A fine lady brings them,
Luxury-lap things.
She is sleek too.

What are they doing,
Dogs are not allowed?
This fine lady is allowed
And of course her pets.
How in this place?

You see that old woman
Crumpled in a corner bed,
Ulcers on her cheek?
The fine lady sleek as silk
Comes from Montserrat:
A mansion by the sea
Terraced with sea-grapes.
She's purchased beauty.
Two different lives ago
This old auntie minded her.

Favours are bestowed now,
New clothes and drugs.
Old woman nods and nods and nods.
The little dogs jump and yap,
Pink tongues lick her oozing cheek.
The fine lady cries.
Old auntie smiles and nods
She puts up a hand again
Shoo, shoo, dry the tears
She dried a thousand times
Time gone like forty years.

White Grip

At first you couldn't see her beauty:
This young girl was too-too thin,
Bones were too near the skin:
Where could the blood find room to move?
No soft bosom, just nipples on a chest.
Look hard again, you see it soon:
No beauty ever matched hers in this room.

Oh, it is sad, sad to tell her story;
She did not expect to be here for long.
A man who went away has now come back:
They are matched, she will go with him.
The day she cannot wait for comes along,
She sits for hours combing out her hair.

He walks in and you know: nothing for her there.
He sits, her eyes fasten on his face;
His lips make up a smile, he scorns this place.
Eyes slip and slide from early on:
Five minutes, he turns to check a noise,
Ten, the first look at his golden Seiko watch.
Meanwhile she hungers, devours all of him.
His well-fed frame is squirming all about:
He's embarrassed, how quick he can get out?
Half an hour, it's his time to go, not hers:
Her lustrous eyes cannot, cannot believe it.
It's a simple thing: he made it, she has not.
He quite roughly puts aside her hand,
She grasps his arm most desperately.
No good asking how it ended
With any hope that all went well:
He went away, she died one day.

Some things once glimpsed remain mind-set:
Moon-blaze on an Essequibo shore;
Hawks riding high above this waiting place;
How once a boy looked at Orion's Belt;
An old man crying in the Silver Chapel.
White grip on his arm I can't forget,
Anyway not yet, not yet.

Stone Fish

Abel Washington is eighty-four:
He's the oldest one in here;
Life has finished with him completely.
His mouth dribbles open all day long,
Eyes have clouded the colour of the sea.
The only time he lifts his head a little:
When ice-cream comes for him to suck.
Hard to find his story when I checked:
He has disappeared before his death.
Booker Wharfinger for fifty years
In the old days when sugar sailed in sacks.
No family left at all, all dead or gone away.
Lives condensed like this is history.

Two things alone stick out for me.
He made a famous river swim
Across the Essequibo mouth and back;
And he was known as "Stone Fish" in the town;
It's a mystery: no one now knows why.
I try to ask him, but he makes no reply,
Then take his hand and sit by him
And talk about his Essequibo swim.
A sudden thing, his hand no longer slack
His eyes come level, his head unsags
For a second, for the briefest shiver.
What happened? What came back?
Is nothing lost, did he feel the river?

Amerindian

I suppose you'd say with truth
No one here looks all that "right".
But they settle themselves down.
He was all wrong from start to finish;
He squatted in his bed half the time
Paddling a strange bateau.

All his life he knew forests,
Forests and the great rivers.
Why bring him in town to die?
His soul is damned that way.
Tribal over-arching heaven
Replaced by rag of sky.

He should have been with brothers,
He should have died with jaguars and stars
And a wind rising in the trees.
A last wood-fire comforting
The coming on of cold.

Dream for him a savage vision:
A multitude of years will pass
When buildings in this upstart town
Again are lost in sea-drowned grass.
The forest will stay,
Nothing he loved gone down.

Ward Weather

The right day to die on:
A grey sky leaking rain,
Colour washed out of everything.
Whole week it's like this,
Trees groaning in the sea-wind,
Mornings sad after black nights.
Can't blame people dying today!

Last week it was different:
Humming-bird sort of weather.
Sun flaming in the sky,
Rose-smell, hot grass, and ripening pomegranates,
At night stars crackling like sparks from a fire.
In here people died then too!

Draw no conclusions from the outside weather.
Rain or bright shining sun
Ward weather is Ward weather.
I recall the sorrow of all graves
And what the old men say:
What a day to die on
Is any day!

A Row About the Moon

Regular as religion, every month,
There is a row about the moon.

When the full moon comes to flower
It floods the earth with silver colour.
A basin of white water spills and froths
And slops all over the town.
A bright pallor spreads in dark corridors.

Some in Mercy Ward complain:
They hate and fear the great white ghost
That makes them think of Jumbie-birds.
They want the tall blinds pulled across:
Keep out the coffin-colour, these ones say,
Keep out the leper-shine,
This fungus-staining of our skin.

Some want the moon let in:
They like the pallid beauty everywhere,
The waxen light of lilies that it throws.
Throw the windows wide and let her in,
The grey fox of the night, our pet,
We may not see again, so sleek, so silvery,
Let her in!

Caged

The stroke stuns him into just a stare:
Mouth screams without a scream being there.
Neck muscles tighten, throat-apple thrums.
Plucks with fingers at his lips and tongue
To rip out songs or words or anything,
He strains and sweats to say a single word.
Paradise would be to let out half a cry:
Nothing comes; his eyes rage.
Think of birds that can no longer fly:
His skull is like a bolted cage,
No opening anywhere.
The slightest motion, a shivering in the cheek
Like wings in flutter before flight.
No further movement comes:
Inside there alone, alone, alone, alone,
Wings nailed right through to bone.

Sweet Pepper Sunday

Hook-nosed Amoroso,
Eyes blazing,
Spade beard bristling white,
Demanded the right
To better food.
Slop and sausages
Were not his fare,
So he said,
And made it clear
He wanted action.
A buzz arose:
Rebellion in the air!
He wasn't just ignored,
He had a victory:
On Sunday, the Ward
Served, on special china,
Red sweet peppers
Stuffed with garlic crab.
Worth remarking,
This Conqueror of Drab.
Not often did you see
Such cookery.
Somebody skylarking!
But Amoroso,
Eyes blazing,
In the humming Ward
Lifted up his fist
In triumph
To the Lord!

The Lament of "Big Bull" Cousins

Tell me the truth!
This could be me?
God loose me in the world
To love women
And women to love me back.
How this could be me!
So maugre and wrinkly-looking,
So mash-up in misery?

Something inside eating me up
Sitting crawly like a slug-king
Taking what it want when
Shrinking up everything.
It like most what most fresh,
Sucking the brain, drawing down the flesh.
It shrivel up the good, thick loins,
It hollow out my jouncy cheeks
Mek big-barrel chest like a little biscuit.
It fattening up fat inside:
Everything else getting trembly and thin.
Years and years it eat and eat
Now it nearly finish and done
Like it want to eat up everything.
It starting East, it going West
Soon it going leave alone by itself
And only the heart in the breast,
Then that eat too and all done!

Skin shine once like silk, man,
Smooth like pure molasses flow
Not a mark on this black man.
Muscle in my belly-pit
Hard as stone, not a fat-ounce:
Knock it, your hand bounce.
Who could mock me,
Match my mastery?

Now look at me good!
This could be me?
Eye never see glass until sixty,
Could sight the old chimney up the coast
From so far like a close-up post:
While people straining, I laughing and reading.
Clear-clear eye, storm-sea grey
Now everything gone and fade away.
Eye full of pink string and boo-boo
Who could play joke so? Who?

Who is it abuse me so?
How who it is could ben' so low?
You could tell why it is,
Why He it is allow this wickedness,
Bitter-bitter after so much sweetness?
I fresh and spright and young,
Next day donkey-drop-dung!
Why life can't fix up a different way?
Why night have to follow bright day?
It could have been organise so
You getting greater as you go:

First is sour, then is spice,
The direction is to Paradise.
So why it couldn't be all we fate
To end up young and bright and straight
From old and scrawny and wither and grey?
It could damn well be fix up that way!

A big, brawly man I was
Big everywhere I tell you,
Big down there too:
Ask any women I know.
Now look how I scrawly!
How this could be so?
There wasn't a woman in town
Didn't know my renown:
Every night
They testing my might.
I teking my pick
When one done, I ready fo' next:
Night have no woman, I vex!
How these days done so quick?

But one woman this heart beat fo' still
I think she dead now forty years.
Sweet, sweet as morning wind
Oh Lord, Lord, she drink like wine!
Eye get heavy with hold-back tears
Watch me now, so dry-up and old
She lucky bad she never get old.
Out of so much she was my One
How quick-and-go that sweet time done.

You could tell me what sense it make
To build something good only fo' break?
I don't understand this big mystery:
A priest-man say it is God decree!
Before I done I going have my say,
Cuss I going cuss, not pray I pray:
I going cuss this God before I die
And He ent have no reason to ask me why.

A *Leopard in the Sky*

In October
On pure moonless nights
There is a leopard in the sky.

Above the black outline of trees
Amidst the thousand glittering stars
I trace the daring of its leap.

Night after night
At sea in the terrible boat
He saw the leopard burning in the stars.

Bound from Calcutta
To the sweet green plantations
Gopaul Singh, grown old, remembers only this.

He died here yesterday.
Forever he has made me see
A leopard burn and leap among October stars.

Thorn Bush

One day a corn-bird, flash of gold,
Got caught in the thorn bush outside.
Something happened: a bird should know bushes.
An old lady saw it from the Ward:
It worried her, she made a great upset.
Brisk Nurse Guyadeen went down herself,
Got out the bird and threw it free:
It soared above the mango trees.
The old lady grew pleased, quieted down.
Not such a big event, you'd say.
For some reason I recall that day:
The corn-bird fluttering in the thorn;
I was forty and the world seemed old.

God's Work

Mister Edwards, more my good friend
Than gardener and handyman at home,
Served me well for half my life.
Prince, they called him, born about that colonial time:
I called him Mister Edwards until the hour he died.

Strong black face, handsome old man,
Ashy cap of curled short hair,
Never sick a day until a day he sick.
"Wind by the heart," he said
But the heart was sound, too sound,
It took months of agony to kill him
Ripping his guts away slowly
Until that strong, good man was nothing.

"God's work," he would say
When the rain pelted down
And floods rushed in the rivers
And storms lashed the tree-tops.
And "God's work" now he said
When the pain wracked him
Spasms crumpling up his face
Sweat dripping in the effort to hold back
The gut-contracting cry not quite escaping.
"Prince Edwards, he too strong for cry,"
But his last day in my arms he cried.
"God's work!"
God should play more.

Calypso

Here is not for emergency
But sometimes there is overflow
And they have to bring them in:
Like this pretty girl in pretty party dress
And tall, young, handsome smashed-up man.
You can tell it's month-end Friday night
Money in his pocket, a girl to court,
After rum and dancing, show-off time:
80 down the avenue by the old train-line,
Life good, the wind sweet.
They're ugly now, butcher's meat.

Try of course, hustle about,
But they're dying, nothing to do;
They're completely out of place too.
They make the Ward restless
Barging in, no patience, such a mess.
Dying has rhythms, fast and slow:
The Ward is waltzing, they calypso.

The Cancer

Strange case.
Rich, debonair, and completely with-it
Young Whittaker, the lawyer,
He got cancer and would die.
They made no bones about it,
Opened him and shut him up again,
Told him he had three months, no more.

He took it well, you never know who will:
Straightened all his business with his wife,
Set up a Trust for John Whittaker, his son,
Drank the best malt whisky while he could,
Played the hero part to absolute perfection.
The sun will boil the earth in any case.

Then he seemed to go a little mad:
He checked himself in here, in Mercy Ward.
Understand, this is for the poorest of the poor
And Whittaker was on his way to being very rich.
He came in alone, not even with his wife,
Signed the forms, and settled in his bed:
Visitors who came were most embarrassed.
No plea could budge him; his end came here.
I never found the reason out for sure.
(Whoever finds a reason that is sure?)
Turning up the records when he died
I found another Whittaker, named John,
Died in Mercy seven years before.

I puzzled at it, not for long:
Why dig for agonies that are gone?
It lies too near the desperate human heart
To tell for sure how sons and fathers part.

Bird-Song

Sky, colour of agouti, drips rain,
A strong wind blows in the gulls from the sea.
Young boy in a blue jacket, head hunched,
Bicycles in carrying a pan of milk.

Every morning he comes without fail.
The pan clanks against the bike's side:
It's for his grandmother in Mercy Ward.
The sound wakens me like bird-song.

Love Affair

At four precisely every afternoon,
She starts preparing for the visitor.
She smooths the sheets and tidies up all round:
Her house to keep has narrowed down to this.
She dresses carefully and puts sweet talcum on,
Grey hair she combs as much as can be combed,
And settles in her chair, folds her hands and waits.
Her day, her life, concentrated in this hour:
Her eyes intently turn towards the opened door.

At five precisely every afternoon
He comes in through the door at visiting hour.
His suit is shiny-old but pressed and clean.
He takes off an old beret on entering the Ward,
He leans quite heavily upon a worn-wood cane.
Without fail he shyly gives a wave towards her bed,
Then slowly stumps towards her and she looks content.

Quietly they sit together near the tidy bed:
They hardly speak a word the whole hour he is here.
She bends a little closer, he gives a half-way smile.
She rocks a while and he relaxes.
But there is something in the closeness of the chairs:
Strangers would be further, even friends not half so near.
They doubly occupy a single space in time:
That space is empty if he for one's not there.

At five to six he rises from his usual place.
She looks at him, he gives her half a nod
And bends stiffly down and touches her old cheek
And takes her hand in his and she takes his:
No words exchanged, and that is all there is.
At exactly six o'clock, when visiting hour ends,
He goes towards the door and does not turn at all.
Her sadness deeper than our customary sorrow,
She turns away and yearns towards tomorrow.

The Place They Have To Go

When someone checks into Mercy Ward
One of the particulars you have to get
Is what provision has been made
For a burial costing nothing, net.
They look restless and turn away.
Even if you have a few days only
You don't want to think of the black hearse
Pulled by the half-blind City horses
Or about Merriman's fourth best limousine
Rattling unattended through the streets.
And you don't want to know
About that part of the graveyard
Where no flowers grow, just tussocky grass
And nettles and black-ant nests.

You often have to visit where they go:
A bare field where goats are grazed,
Rust-coloured grasshoppers whirring as you step.
Across the way the splendid tombs arise
White and shaded by huge impressive trees:
Marble blossoms deck them down the years.
And ornaments and wreaths in perfect alabaster.
But here of course no monuments arise:
Graves dug in line straight into earth.
When freshly dug slap-dash dirt-mounds show
With wooden crosses stuck awry on top:
Rain crumbles them shapeless in a month or so.
This field of grass and goat-weed
Holds a bare and hopeless dignity.

The Supervisor's office is a simple place:
A chair, a desk, a concrete vault
Where archives of all burials are kept;
The leather-covered volumes stretch centuries back.
It sets things in perspective right away:
The record is equal in these careful books,
Inscribes for all an austere common fate.
No space for high or space for low:
The line of written detail does not change,
All are put down here the same,
Bare, unblemished soul-mates, row on row.
In the field you do not get to see
The part of burial that does not show
Obscurity or utmost fame:
The scene below is much the same.

Blue Potaro Hills

Old Oudit Ram seemed, to those who knew,
To have taken up permanent residence
In the coveted corner bed on the Western side.
He had even accumulated a few belongings,
A litter of small items to grace his stay,
A sort of shrine to give a sort of meaning
To his sort of life: a holy Hindu picture, a tattered book,
A bag of stones (I don't know why), a faded Panam bag.
He seemed to have settled in for good, or bad,
And he behaved himself and said his prayers and ate.

Without any warning, at evening time one day,
He surprised the Ward by getting up and walking out.
He showed every sign of knowing what he did,
Collecting up his picture, book, and rocks,
And also his small bag, and making for the door.
He got quite far, almost to the stairs outside
Before the shouts brought order back again,
And he was hustled back to stay in bed
Where he belonged, the nurses told him scoldingly,
And not where he was trying hard to go,
As he explained: home, home, one time more,
Home, far away and far to go,
Home where he remembered in the evening mist
Blue Potaro hills of young days long ago.

Praise Song for Mary

Rounded
O of love
boon of heaven
heavy-looking now
birth soon to come
I celebrate the joy
beauty of body-swell
oval paradisal
proud miracle
I celebrate
all soft and circling forms
earth-root and flower
the golden pregnant moon
showers shadows
call-glory of carols
bowls of ripe oranges
rose mangoes full plums too
stuffed sweet melons
rotund sun-ball in the sky
fat cloud-bellies sailing
in looms and loops of light
smoke-mist over water
rain curves on river
ocean-swoops billows
roses pools of moon-water
home home home.

Hollows look hallowed
they are the kin of hoops
fat loaves –
hot bounty

from old stoves
noontime and swallows
arcs of light
you are buoyant with becoming
a fountain
a meteor shower
flower-bloom
my burgeoning love
rock and cradling stars
in your belly-dark
time booms
and throbs and towers
life starts again
I hear the double-heart
that God made and me
and you will make me soon
a high-shining son.

My Father's Prayer Book, Page 44

Most life is ice-melt,
bells through sea-mist,
dark coming home and hurrying.
There are no exceptions.
Thoughtful men feeling
the stars' pull across half the world,
knowing coasts' thick rocks
vanish in the seas' wash finally –
these men too have urgent private business:
they deal in golden things and lures.

Faded writing in a prayer book's margin –
this remedy for love affairs and projects:
"Stand under old trees in the wind."
Heaven is huge then and not temporary.

Gifts for a Farewell

Koetsu, famous for his tea-bowls,
mainly black, others rufous or turkey-wattle red,
some splashed with white as from an eagle's droppings:
his glazing holds a brightness like fireflies.
Eighteen tea-bowls that he made are left.
All the rest are gone, thousands they say;
the centuries have stamped them all to pieces.
I wish you this gift, a bowl so baked and spun.

Farmers in vivid scarlet clothes
till strawberry fields in Pougastel.
A wild wind haunts that Breton coast
where fish-boats bring in their silver catch.
Honoured for beauty, I have read,
you must walk in Pougastel.

In Mexico the Tarascans long ago
made mosaics from the wings of birds.
Most famous of all villages in this art
Tzintzuntzan on a golden lake –
in Mayan meaning "tresses of the day-star".
They worked thus: drop by drop an orchid's glue
bound gold-green feathers into tapestry.
May you seek and love such wonders all your life.

These gifts for you, Philip O'Meara,
friend of the good hours, you would like to know
these things and you will treasure them
and yet reflect how simply beauty falls
and the dark comes and hearts slow.
You who dance upon the ice
have always known what dwells below.

Any Poem

You can make a poem about anything.
In fact, that would be the first line of it:
About life, how it passes
About death, how it comes
About beauty, how it lasts
While it lasts
About love, which is a strong thing
But strong things break
About the old lady in lace
Who lived a hundred years
And is forgotten
About home, which is bright
About great men, who wear out
Quicker than stones
About truth which is fidgety
And will not stand still
About eternity, which time contains
About God, who invented Himself
Like a poem.

Poems, late 1980s and after

A White Man Considers the Situation

Perhaps it is time to retreat from these well-loved shores.
The swell heaves on the beach, angry clouds pile:
The surf is ominous, storms are coming.
I see I am a tourist in my own land:
My brutal tenancy is over, they all say,
The centuries have faded like a dream ...

Every day it is harder for the timid to make plans,
People do not say good morning with the former politeness.
The pavements feel safe only when old men pass.
The grip of power slides away, slides.
Something is missing in days still filled with pleasure;
There is emptiness, dreaming in the air.
Where ruling ends, the ruler cannot stay:
A diminished mastery is the keenest woe.

The best measure is the use of time.
My father's father planted once
A green tree in this quiet garden:
It was to yield ancestral wood
To grace my grandson's christening chair.

The best measure is the use of time.
I decorate now my dark-skinned love
With hibiscus for her shining hair
The petals fade, the sun burns out
Red hibiscus in her shining hair.

I lie sleepless in the embroidered sheets,
A sprig of khus-khus scents the room.
The night is dark with cloud, and lonely.
The black sentries are whispering, restless.
My father heard a hurricane of nightingales
Once upon a time, once upon a time.
Now the owl hoots, signalling danger coming,
The moon is half alight, throwing coldness.

There is no way back, no forward way;
My heart grows clenched from inner grief.
Almost certainly I will have to go from here.
The laagers of the world build higher, black and white.
And no one is to blame except my brother, me.
No one is to blame except my brother.

River Grave

Near giant bogwood that blunts axes
Half-buried in a moon-filled place
They dug up chanced-upon grey bones,
Cluster of dog-grey bones, shining,
Out of gold and river mud,
Heavy, glittering, golden, clinging,
Old as mountains, there, looming black,
Far away, far in the mist,
The ominous, unsheltering sky.
Slippery as fish, silvery as river-fall,
In the bag that carried them to camp
The grey bones sang and danced and clattered.
Men the colour of honey and black iron:
One man hung a grey bone on his chest,
One man carved a grey bone for a flute,
One man boiled a grey bone for his soup
To sup miracles, to gain the ancient thing,
One man with a grey bone called the rain
To rage, to scour the gold down quick.
And camp-men used the grey bones left,
Made music with those clattering bones:
Hit hard at midnight all together
Clack-clack, ringing, clack-clack, singing
Strange echo, clack-clack, strange floating moon:
Old gold men dance and dance and dance
And dance, until old bones all-a-tremble,
They fall down, watch the bones still clatter-sing.
Whose grave was dug a thousand years
He must have been a music man.

Life and Death Tree

Along the dark, lonely river
Silent as leaf-drift
An opening in the cliff of white quartz:
A grove of dead-looking trees
Stark in the burning sun.

Out of black, bare sticks
Velvet-white blossoms spring:
The life-and-death tree.
Green leaves will sprout from it
As bright flowers die.
The scent of the gold-centred flowers
Pours out of the live and dead grove.

Four girls from the yam farm,
They are preparing a sister's wedding.
They throw up stones in the branches
Accurately shaking down the blossoms.
Their clothes are coming down too.
The dips of their navels fill with sweat,
Gleaming drops run down like diamonds.

Nearby, the stink of a killing place:
Black flies, bright knives.
Gleaming with sweat too
Three boys gutting fish
Marvel and fidget.

Dream Island

Far up from the ocean coast,
Green-deep in Essequibo forest,
For briefest season –
Soon as fast-water comes, it will go –
The tides have tugged an island into being.
A blazing, bone-white beach
Appears mid-river, sudden as a dream:
Bank of sand and scoured stones,
Pink shells from prehistoric seas.
Low-tide you can land
And own this silent, lovely place.
Clear, red water lapping past,
Sea-birds alighting, preening:
The sounds of wings and water.
A great sky of piling clouds
And winds that are the breath of God:
Wide, amazing, perfect stillness.
I come ashore through gleaming water
Bringing a feast of gold-red berries,
Cassava bread, flowers for beauty
That will last an hour.
I come to read on this bright temporary island
The Overture to Proust's beloved book.
Heat-lightning flashes in far mountains:
Storms will soon wash all this away.
Lost, lost in the great river of this book!
Clouds of fireflies burn as night begins:
No one will ever do what I have done.

Scholar

The forest clears, socket of silence
In the huge green shout of trees:
Weather-greyed chapel, box-small, closed,
Dogs snarl and snap on long ropes
Round scarlet-blossomed trees.
My voice ripping the noon-day air
Summons the friar, frail as dried leaves.
Old age stoops him like a crescent,
One eye glass-white, skull clean-boned,
Teeth broken-black, his robe of threadbare blue.
He has never come down river.

There is no greater mystery than any man.
I see the old books I have come to see:
Shelves upon shelves in thousands once,
Latin histories, old maps, testaments and laws,
Thick books of traveller's tales and governments.
They all were brought from Heidelberg and Rome:
"A wild, green place for books,"
He gestures in the lustrous air.
"It seemed a good thing to be done.
I meant to write." He shrugs it off.
The books are crumbling, tumbled out of place,
Worm-holed, rat-eaten, damp-decayed.
They will go soon to dust like men.

I am allowed the old priest's journal:
Ten marvellous notebooks two thousand pages long,

Lined, yellowing paper half-a-century old.
I turn to April eighteenth, nineteen thirty-three:
"Rain fell night-long and in the morning
Gold-billed toucans skimmed the trees."

The last note is five years back,
No more after. The old man shrugs again.
"To see the moon-blaze in the trees
Perfect itself. A clearer sight of God."
The entries end. The rest is blank.
Dust drifts in the warm, illumined air,
The shuttered room is still. He prays.

"Hangman" Cory

When the launch sank off Fort Island
People were drowning in the black mud
Bawling out "Oh God! Oh God!"
God did not come. It was like any day,
Sun shining on wind-rippled river,
Except men were struggling and dying,
Women and children choking in the mangrove roots.
People were running on the shore and calling
"Oh God! Oh God!" How God could come?
God can't mind everyone.
But look at this now! Look at story!
"Hangman" Cory arrive like God.
Let me tell you Hangman's story.

Nathaniel Cory once loved a lady
She was a wanton lady, she used him badly.
His mind stop work when he see her beauty:
He was a puppy-dog in her company,
People laugh at "kiss-she-foot-bottom" Cory.
This wanton lady take another man one day,
Open, brazen, she parade before Nathaniel Cory,
Laugh and say for all to hear clearly
How this man was the sweetest man for she,
How Cory never, never could satisfy she,
Nathaniel Cory stay quiet all the long day
Night came and when the man lay with the lady
Cory walked in open so, easily, terribly,
Lash both two with his sharp timber-axe fiercely
Cut them in pieces like red melons on a tray.
When judge-man say she provoke the jealousy
And Cory get only five years off his liberty
"No! No! No! No!" shouted Nathaniel Cory,
"She be life, my love, my beauty,
I have to go to hell with she, my life, my beauty.
She only gone in front of me.
Hang me by the neck to die gladly,
Hang me high, high and quickly!"
The people whispering make it legendary:
It so he get the name of "Hangman" Cory.

Off Fort Island that bright morning
Was he who God send to save the people.
People bawling on the black stelling for a saviour,
They never expect to see "Hangman" Cory come.
He live so quiet among them all the years,
Minding a pumpkin patch behind the white Chapel,
He smoke his thorn pipe, never say one word.

There he stood on the black stelling like a God.
Bibi La Fontaine, ice-pick thin and hard,
Fifty years trading plantain along the river coast,
Recount what happen that bright morning in her life.
Launch just left the Fort to go Parika side,
Deep inside boat-belly a thunder-sound was heard:
Time flicker, in a second, in a cat-wink,
Boat gone bottom. How quick it was:
She belched a warm beer she was drinking,
Before the belch belch good the boat capsize and gone.
"Under I go, the whole boat on top of me:
Mud yellow dim my eyes, cold log brace my heart.
I see my little Fancy who die fifty years gone by,
And then I see for sure is the monster death that come.
And my mind saying why an old woman should struggle so,
Let me go, and still I fighting not to go
And there is Fancy, the little one, crying in my arms.
A rough hand come and choke me round the neck
And pull me where I done pin good in mud.
This man had come for me in the dark water,
He find me like a miracle and take me safe ashore:
Sun so bright, earth hard, I hear a singing bird.
Never morning wind feel so sweet, you hear I give my word."

"Hangman" dive and dive in the dark water.
Everyone like they turn to stone but he:
Women bawling and running and pointing trembly
Big men shouting and doing nothing foolishly.
Only "Hangman" Cory doing the work of God.
And everytime he come up with another one
As if God guide him in the mangrove mud.
A score he save and still he went for more
Coming up with weed-tendrils round his head

And wound around his throat like gallow's rope.
He delivering up children from the river-womb,
His eyes staring red and cold and terrible,
Not one word he said in all his glory.

These are the plain facts about "Hangman" Cory,
His day of evil, his day of glory:
He cut his beauty up like a red melon in the market;
God send him one day to save the drowning people.
Time will sort the meaning of all this out:
The hunting moon will rise one last, appalling, time
And he will come to rest like all men come to rest.
Though years pass, men should know his story:
"Oh God! Oh God!" the people call and God send
    "Hangman" Cory.

Perfect Roses

The belching saw-mill half-falling in the river
Stinks of steam, pulped wood, and acrid smoke:
It's near the hut which sells the axe-helves.
Far and holy, the stars control our fate.
The full-bellied lumberman scratches at his balls.
The slattern woman by his side,
Kimono slipping down a caved-in chest,
Slings a snot-nosed infant on her hip.
The yard-space slops with mud and chicken shit,
A cur kicked half to death whines in a corner.
They walk me to where he carves the axes
And where it seems she tends a garden:
Patch of ground, fenced with well-nailed wood,
Black earth neatly forked, packed with shining blooms
Sunset-red, and gold, and white as quartz from Pomeroon.
The pattern of a life is fixed:
Nothing prepared me for the perfect roses.

Nightscape

Thin moon over water
Far thunder on the breeze
Eel-lights through river-mist
Cassiopeia caught in the trees.

Another part of history
A mad prince ruled the age,
At night each star he counted
A throat was cut in rage.

In time the world turns over
See! The prince sinks on his knees
The moon outlines his holy shape,
The star-entangled trees.

Explorer

Here men you meet are strange wayfarers:
   To find a tree that flowers blue in late October,
   Grasshoppers thumbnail small and crimson-winged,
   And ants that smell of citronella.
   Track streams that spring from black-rock shelves
   Aswim with parrot-eyed, ghost-white piranha.
   Trade with men who make the stonewood boats
   And carve amulets that look like pictures in a cave
   That scholars say go back ten thousand years.
A day I saw king-vultures soar higher than the clouds
A man came by and stopped and told his story.
   He searched for the lost Amazons.
   Soft English life, brilliant time at University,
   Rich family, smooth progress to the top,
   Then he read about the Amazon,
   The endless river and its secret tales.
   A myth had now possessed him wholly
   Gaunt, charred-brown, eyes like blue stones in a river:
   Ten years he'd roamed in every Southern forest.
While the howler monkeys roared
Like a wind through mountain passes,
He told the many tales he had pursued
To find the brave women without one breast.
   "I heard this tale of men-despising women
   They danced their men asleep and flew away:
   As they fly they clutch red peppers in their hands
   And pelt blindness down as the men pursue.
   Never to return,
   Never to return to their ancestral sway.
   Never to return.
   In a magic city they yearn and yearn forever.

They live a thousand years and one,
    Their vaginas turn to twittering birds."
Next morning in a cold and crystal pool,
Edged with flowing white mimosa,
Drinking cashew juice and sucking bitter plums,
Before departure when the sun was high and bright,
I asked him what the route was he would go.
    "A white horse's tail has brushed my face
    It is a sign I will succeed one day.
    Their sacred flutes will play for me
    And I will come across their place:
    Palms stand on guard with blackest thorns
    Long as a grand-aunt's knitting needles.
    A lake where all the gold veins run:
    It is not near,
    It is not far,
    The Mirror of the Ancient Moon."
Mad as a torn shoe on a burning road,
Chaste as the stone I toss from hand to hand:
The beauty of God in every thing and man.
Gave him for his quest all he may ever need:
Onions, sugar, salt, and fishing line and love.

Snail Painting

Cold-pale eyes, pale hair, gold-pale skin:
He must have ventured from an icy land.
Once upon another time for Sven Neilson
A pure, freezing country in the North
Must have been his stone-cold home.
Twenty years of wandering brought him far
To frontier river-town, deep in forest country,
Mud-drowned in late December, dusty hot in May.
Down a side street off Bartica main square
He runs a rumshop where bush-whores and gold-men come,
Serves behind the counter and knows them all by name.
He likes the customers to dance; claps his hands,
Jumps and jives in his blue dungarees.
I've been there and suddenly he'll stop
To play Mahler and Walcott's 'Joker' on the box.
He keeps green leafy branches fresh all around the shop.

One night he closed the bar down early,
Beckoned me to stay and led me in the back.
A long room lit by lanterns set on barrels down each side,
Casting gold-black shadows on a strange display:
Long, unrolled sheets of black cloth tacked on frames
Nailed to rough gilt trestles four feet tall.
Eagerly and soberly he explained it all to me:
It filled his inner life, it was important art.
From a jute sack, one of the bundles in a corner,
Soaked in water, earth-encrusted, tied with golden ribbon,
He dipped both hands in and pulled out a score of snails:
Gleamed white and pale blue in the lantern light.

He put them on the black cloth one by one
At all the corners. We watched their silver scrawls.
He demonstrates most carefully, anxious to explain.
The slow trails glow, meander, cross and multiply:
The tangled veins of silver make maps he can decipher.
The craft is where he spaces out the snails along
    the frames.
The largest works use up a hundred snails or more:
The black cloth glows in complex mastery.

At first he used to mark the movements on the cloth
To make precise record for painting on huge canvases
Stored for years, vast elaborate scrolls slashed with all
    the colours.
His soul being not at rest, he destroyed them all:
The snails alone are now enough for him.
He sees no greater art or act than this:
Such silver beauty, tracings straight from God.
Whole nights he sits and looks in wonder:
Immortal patterns forming in his mind,
Paths of peace and trackless wastes of war.
When daylight comes the silver marks are gone:
The day's first customers wait outside for rum.

Deep Pool

Just past that boat-killer, Sansom's Cataract,
Which boils the water white for half a mile
And takes the river ten levels down –
In a funnel of dark and green-mossed rock
Overhung with giant vine-entangled trees
So that no sun ever lights the gloom
Lies Deep Pool, cold and black as witches' bracelets.
A ledge of rock overlooks the still and crystal pool:
There's no hand-hold to be got down there
Should you be thrown or dive. The rock is sheer,
Slimed with water oozing like cold sweat
Upon the slippery moss and lichen-covered walls.
The drip of water in that silent place is ominous,
Sometimes you hear low sighs like women moaning.

A flower thrown in that water sinks like stone:
A skull will bob and float and grin.
From the tall ledge drop a severed jaguar's head
It will descend the black depths for a day,
Be cast up again with jewels in its fleshless eyes.
Let down a rope tall as all the forest's trees
It will never plumb those hideous depths
That have no limits known to puny man.
The taste of its black water strangles cowards.
Bring maidens late in bleeding there,
They will gush blood like a fountain.
Before ever man wrote down his pain
But carved it on enduring rock
The purpose of this place was plain:
Since angry Gods must be appeased
Here were they made promises and pleased.

A visiting scientist made precise surveys,
Succinctly described the properties of the pool,
Measured it exactly twenty fathoms deep
Which makes it deep, he wrote, but not mysterious.
Found nothing in it to account for miracles:
No dye, piranha, alkaline, or poison.
Strange sounds heard sometimes by the river-men
Explained by wind sighing through rock-fissures
    hidden near:
A plaintive noise, of course, but nature made it so.
He was content to note, in summing up his paper,
That myths dismantled were his stock-in-trade:
He dealt in facts, not dreams and tales of men.

Deep Pool never gets the sun
And yet the moon is welcomed there.
The pale spectre of the moon is dear
To such places which shadows never leave,
Shadows that are made by more than suns:
Agony, horror, hate, and fear,
Not reached by measurement, are there.

Forest Path, Nightfall

Paths cut last month to open up new timber
Are lit with streams of late slanting sun:
Beneath a canopy of green crowns of mora trees
Shadows gather except where float tall pillars
Of thick golden light that sets the green dark shining.
So evening falls, I walk this forest path,
Shadowy nave of an immense cathedral:
When Chartres is finest dust, this still will stand,
It stretches far, never-ending in its beauty,
Shines with its own green and gold-stained glass.
When a wind comes the stained windows shiver
A myriad alternating, dark then gleaming, pieces
That never reach the floor but float suspended,
Shimmering arcs of velvet-black and emerald.
One mile from here I found, below its cleansed white beak,
A swarm of ants eating the entrails of an eagle.
Night-shadows begin to rise, mist shaken
From hidden censers in this holy place.
Stars and fireflies, candles lit by ancient priests,
Fill the huge cavern with glowing taper-lights.
In childhood even joy seemed permanent:
I feel cold as if earth was cathedral-stone
Chilled for centuries before the age of man.
In this immense god-theatre night after night brings on
A sense of never-ending mystery vast as time
That swallows man, all his art and legends.
You cannot walk in great forests without diminishment.

The Sun Parrots Are Late This Year

for Chico Mendez, murdered Brazilian Environmentalist

The great forests of the world are burning down,
Far away in Amazon they burn,
Far beyond our eyes the trees are cut
And cleared and heaped and fired:
Ashes fill the rivers for miles and miles,
The rivers are stained with the blood of mighty trees.
Great rivers are brothers of great forests
And immense clouds shadowing the rose-lit waters
Are cousins of this tribe of the earth-gods
Under the ancient watch of the stars.
The forest dwindles; it will soon be nothing,
Shrubs sprouting untidily in scorched black earth.
The sun will burn the earth, before now shadowed
For a hundred thousand years, dark and dripping,
Hiding jewelled insects and thick-veined plants,
Blue-black orchids with white hearts, red macaws,
The green lace of ferns, gold butterflies, opal snakes.
Everything shrivels and dust begins to blow:
It is as if acid was poured on the silken land.

It is far from here now, but it is coming nearer,
Those who love forests also are cut down.
This month, this year, we may not suffer:
The brutal way things are, it will come.
Already the cloud patterns are different each year,
The winds blow from new directions,
The rain comes earlier, beats down harder,
Or it is dry when the pastures thirst.
In this dark, over-arching Essequibo forest

I walk near the shining river in the green paths
Cool and green as melons laid in running streams.
I cannot imagine all the forests going down,
The great black hogs not snouting for the pulp of fruit,
All this beauty and power and shining life gone.
But in far, once emerald Amazon the forest dies
By fire, fiercer than bright axes.
The roar of the wind in trees is sweet,
Reassuring, the heavens stretch far and bright
Above the loneliness of mist-shrouded forest trails,
And there is such a feel of softness in the evening air.
Can it be that all of this will go, leaving the
        clean-boned land?
I wonder if my children's children, come this way,
Will see the great forest spread green and tall and far
As it spreads now far and green for me.
Is it my imagination that the days are furnace-hot,
The sun parrots late or not come at all this year?

The River-Crossing Moths

The sun rises on the silent river,
A few bird-calls haunt the morning air,
Mist-tendrils drift among the tops of trees,
The bateau glides slow on the quiet, silver water:
It is a time of peace and solitude,
The dreaming hour before the world awakes.
In a flash a cloud of velvet, shimmering moths,
Black-shining, edged with emerald-white,
Rise marvellously from the sun-touched bank:
They fly in thousands to the far shore.

The wild brilliance, the suddenness, the wonder:
Fathomless parting from all that is secure!
Here the great river is miles wide,
In thousands the shining moths will die.
Their brave fragility cannot last for long:
Already scores have lost the way,
Fall battered, gleaming, in the bateau
And flutter dying on the falling tide,
A destiny fulfilled to end without a trace.
The rising wind will tear their delicacy apart,
The sun will burn them in its great fire,
River-birds will spear them from the sky
For food or sport, or they at last will tire.
Their shredded velvet wings will strew the waters
For a moment, beautiful, then sink like sun-burst bubbles.
Rare and distant from all it knew before,
Will even one reach that green opposing shore?

Strange quest these velvet moths pursued
This silver morning on the great river,
Dared to mount the dangerous, high air
And fly towards the rising flame of sun.
On that far shore for certain there must be
A perfect lure to justify such lunacy,
A trap more potent than any life-force sets,
A poison sweeter than moth-nectar ever gets.
Some fruit of love, some paradisal tree,
In the far forest they discover and are free.

Shadows Will Hide the Sun

for Darren, at the ceremony of baptism

Bathe him in light
I pray, bathe my son in light:
his be a good life's lustre.
Through a world growing dark
every passing hour
bathe him in light.
Let brightness gleam about him;
bitter will be days to come,
shadows will hide the sun.
Thus is the life of man,
but within him let brightness dwell.
Spare him dullness all his days,
defend him ever from despair.
From valley depths
let Heaven lead him;
never lose the mountain light.
Through gall and ash
a pearl will shine:
let his life gleam.
In the dark world
bathe him in light.

White Cathedrals

Five boys swim in the canal,
diving amid white lilies with golden hearts.
Water-shine gleams on their naked bodies,
eel-black beauty in the morning light.

No matter the weight
of the white cathedrals –
barns of heaven,
the massed shops full of goods,
the laugh-shatterers,
the exact and confident sciences,
the thud of marching feet,
nothing that the husked men say
can drown their joy.

My Son Selects a Stone

When he was six and I was fifty-six
all that week-long holiday
my son brought stones from the sea.
What is this? A shark's tooth from the deep.
And these? Leaf of whitened coral.
Wave-worn bottle once held pirate rum.
Crystal from a drowned sailor's chain.
Magenta tile broken from a Great House floor,
a gleam of porcelain treasure-cup.
Snippet of glinting quartz we long pored over.
Are these valuable diamonds, Dad?
He lined them up to show his mother. Proud
cornucopia from the eternal sea. She praised him.

At the end he threw them all away,
kept none of the beautiful, the curious,
the sea-shaped wonders he had found
and brought for our appraisal,
but kept a solid, ordinary, small rock
no different from a scattered multitude
that I could see. He has it still.
He never told us why he kept it.

Betrothal

Old story. Young girl getting bigger now:
fifteen, tender, good, submissive;
parents want the best for her:
pious, fierce for family and name,
and old traditions steeped in race and time.
Goldsmith's son is thirty-four:
had his days, boy, played an eager field,
wants to settle now and take a wife.
Offers house and future safe as gold,
cows and coconuts up Essequibo Coast.
The thing is done, families agree:
a marriage is arranged for all to see,
proud and suitable and good for all
except – she's irremediably locked in tears.
She will not talk to family or friends
except to say she does not wish to live
if this must be the burden of her days:
not furious but a quiet, downward look.

All are summoned against this stubbornness:
old, gentle uncles come, brothers hold her hands,
white-robed pandit shakes his head and warns.
They appeal to me: I see the girl
I knew since parents gave her birth.
She has her story when we sit alone.
Young man she saw once by the temple wall:
hardly speak though they meet at festivals.
Hands once touched, and held, and that's enough.
I say the sensible things I must
but eyes have blazed like that before,
storm-light on a sunless shore.

96

I meet my old, grey, saddened friends.
"She is young! What does she know of life!"

Yes, she is young as the new moon,
green as young grass after rain,
but what she now has in her heart –
hard as antique mountain stone
sleepless, ancient scythe of stars.
And, yes, she will kill herself
should you bring this goldsmith's son of yours.

Bread and Fish Hooks

A friend brought fat loaf-bread
crusty, straight from the oven;
I broke off a piece to eat,
taste of the first heat good.
He brought fish hooks, shining;
we followed a remote path, among stones,
dust gathering on our coats;
fished all day under a sulphur sky.
Returning, we ate a few small fish, roasted,
and the new bread he had given
and cold water from a plain jug.
We talked about the sea,
of other things too, like love,
but mostly about the sea which is large.
At night I had a vision of death:
a shoreline receding forever but always near
and a man walking there, gifts in his hands.

Beaucaillou

The wind blows my mother's thin grey hair;
she speaks of Beaucaillou, her swift horse.
When she was a girl she recalls
the fine horse in his gleaming trap:
the snort and stamp and jingle
and her father laughing, clapping,
shouting, "Home, Beaucaillou, home!"
And the wind blowing in her red, wild hair.

Seen Through Closed Eyes

Mountains hung with dreams;
from the caves, whispers of healing.
Across the onion field
bright berries glow in green trees,
flights of birds
soar below the thunderhead –
sudden circles of light.
Remember how love burns
before flesh and bone are parted.
Faraway, tipsy as Pharaohs,
children shriek with joy.
The noise of time fills my ears
endless as the air.
Fire-falls, the dying of the day,
and then the intensity of the night.

Rain

No rain for months, sky hard blue,
ground hardening like iron,
earth hot to shod feet,
smoke-shawls from bush-fires;
sun glares red before night falls.
White the worst colour, bright as bone.
Time soon coming when the oxen starve;
grass turns to ash, savannahs
send up clouds of burning dust.
Green is a colour gentle and forgotten
like blood gone from a dead face.
Mud cracks in pools once sweet with lilies.

Old men, who have known
the hard seasons, say
water would be the best gift
if it could be wrapped.

And so it comes, a fundamental beauty,
a simple thing not often counted –
like love; when it's there life balances,
though we do not feel the balancing,
until departure leaves us husked and dry.
It comes again and steadies us,
soothing, far away, a noise in the clouds,
a summoning freshness in everything.
An arid heartland springs alive;
water is love; it clears and shines:
clemency for a wracked land.

Archive

One by one the old men die:
the libraries are burning down.
On Lombard Street near Ma Belle's parlour
in a high and rotting house
greyed by time and fungus weather
I find one of the last ones,
a century old, and half alert.
He inhabits a bare, discarded room;
greets me sitting on a single bed.
A quarter candle gives him light;
enamel basins catch the rain.
The food is peppery, the rum is strong.

In a cracked mirror hung askew
I catch sight of my own lines of age.
The shadows carve them dark and deep:
shocked to think I'll follow him so fast.
Nothing keeps; the years defeat us all.
Framed in silver on the bedside table
a picture set to seize the eye:
Sunday dressed and stiffly posed
a small boy holds his father's hand.
When the city tidies up this life,
the silver frame but not the picture
is all that will remain of both.
Decades too late our heroes are acknowledged,
names announced in unattended stations.

Gnarled fingers like black twisted roots
now clutch an ancient bamboo flute.
He plays a twittering, faltering tune;
it peters out and leaves him sad:
"Oh lawd, brain get hard like bone!
Pickle to stone, pickle to stone!"
Stored in his memory are a thousand songs,
now and then he finds them still –
thumps his hand and shouts them out –
and stories for ten shelves of books,
gold chants, cures past numbering,
tinctures from the sap of plants,
lotions, balms from crushed green leaves.
He tells tall tales from Pomeroon:
charms, hunting signs, bull-monsters
from the dark forest, fire witches hung
from starry heavens, tribal flags, and waterfalls –
why they hacked the head off the bone-white ram.

But things are fading fast for him:
recalls exactly how the century turned,
he can't remember yesterday.
I take some notes. But it is sad.
The old man sighs and shakes his head,
hums when he forgets the words.
Nobody keeps old bibles any more.

MacArthur's Life

What happen to old MacArthur
I wonder. They call he Barnyard
when he young, Slim Boy, Hot Cock.
All about town he run, crowing, mounting,
sunlight and morning, stain-sky and night.
It so sweet, why he should bother about anything else?
How a man like he could always find women?
He never pay but he always get. Something, boy,
something in this world; people don't want lonely.
But he get old and begin to fall in trenches.
Women ease he for a while, then drink.
Like he could always find women, he could always
     find drink.

He eye soft, people like he,
he never pick up a stone to pelt.
The years go by so quick, life waste, life done.
The last I see Slim Boy he look groggy
and like he trying something new, I don't know.
Mass finish at Sacred Heart, I see he in a pew
sink on the knee, head bend, one hand shaking.
But that was years ago; I don't know after.

Sing-Song's Place

Sing-Song work forty year in Parkview Club.
Everyone know Sing-Song; he rum-punch famous.
He humming happily when he make the drinks;
everyone know he style, he take good care.
He bother how much ice, perfect measure,
he proudly bring the drinks, as if it matter.
He like to hear compliment; it is he life you know.
He don't know nothing else, he don't want to know.
He share a lifetime with a God he love.
They come with slide-rule and computer, the new people.
Parkview Club change hands; they measuring money.
Sing-Song spilling a few drinks now, he old,
and how he could learn to put a pinch less
when he know the taste going change with that?
Better you put out light in he life.
So he have to go. They knock he off. Who sad?
Redundancy nothing much when dollar value gone.
Well, I hear they closing Parkview down:
computer working good, customer leaving fast.
Why they could never learn true cost?
Sing-Song take it easy, he humming still.
He gone by squatting fields to get a lot.
He build a shanty; it is Sing-Song Place.
Poor people also drink, now they have their prince.

Canticle of the Main Street Madman

The old man blesses stones and men,
a supermarket clerk for years,
they say he has gone mad.
All day he signs the cross on things:
food, trees, earth, and the rubbish trucks.
He stands in Main Street blessing men.
He lifts his eyes towards the sun
blessing that great medallion too.
All night heaven's holy stars are blessed.
I've seen him bend down very low,
give benediction to a lump of shit.

He kneels in rainstorms, blesses them;
bliss lights his mild and streaming face.
Trench lilies red as blood he blesses;
he wades up to his waist in mud.
Birds! Takes a special joy in birds;
they perch or soar, he blesses them
with gestures wide that tell his love.
Stands by the churches during Mass
and signs the cross on celebrants.
Perhaps he means some irony;
he does the same thing at the banks.

What harm does this man do?
All he does is bless the world –
more sane than me or you.
They say he troubles normal men;
it interrupts the train of thought
of busy men, of serious men,
to have this peculiar man intrude

and sign the cross on their backsides.
Degrades the human race, they say.
Who will forgive our sanity?

The only men he will not bless
are policemen. They treat him rough,
come for him, "Main Street disgrace,"
cart him off like roadside rubbish,
bundle him into Brickdam station.
"Cool your blasted arse in there!"
But inside he starts again;
the four walls of his cell are blessed
and any inmates that are near.

He has never tired in his work –
must have blessed the whole of town.
Shakes with age now, soon will die.
Wonder who will take his place?
Who will bless us down the years?
Who will bless the men and stones?
No one will be mad enough to try.
Bless us, Lord, when he has gone.

Mr Perfection

His name was actually that, Manuel Perfection.
The certificate in a slim dossier sets it out:
born in Bartica, Good Friday, nineteen twenty-four,
son of Theodore Perfection and his wife Mathilda.
Schooled by Catholics until the age of twelve –
"A bright boy but rebellious and does not love the Lord."
Then he left "to seek his fortune in the bush."
Laconically a priest records the facts.
The vast forest swallows him for fifty years
and the time has passed like the wind
and the time has passed like a flying cloud
and candle-flies have winked ten times
and soon enough time brought him here.
He died this morning, not pleasantly,
a long time struggling to take a breath
until I, beside him, grew breathless too.

Before me rests the brown folder with his life.
Certificate of birth, baptism card, a school report,
    a letter.
That's all, except the page that ends the file –
sparse list of all he brought in here: bloodstone, knife,
old clothes, a cap; Matron countersigned the list.
The letter dated from thirty years ago,
dirty, scorched with fire, water-marked,
crumpled, it seems, once in an angry fist,
creased so many times it tore in half,
fixed, refixed, with transparent strips of tape.
I read the lines between the scorched-out parts,
guessing words but the sense is plain:

"You deserve the praise of this community
and its children most of all, who thank you."
A village schoolmaster writes the thank-you note.
Such notes in thousands make up our lives
and some keep many and most keep none at all.
"You did the job well, all of us are pleased.
The desks and chairs you constructed to perfection."
I'm sure that word was not deliberate –
the note looks hurried, there are words misspelt.

We all keep things whose value others miss,
shadows of hands that have caressed us.
This is what he culled and kept
and I will keep it too, to remember
how the wind changes and the centuries go
full of meanings we can never know.

Spinster Ganteaume and the Birth of Poetry

Close neighbour of the first home I knew,
gaunt spinster, Bernadette Ganteaume
("On the morrow God will rise again"),
I remember her always in long green dresses,
face bumpy with rosy unerupted boils.
Thick lenses made her pupils hugely bulge:
eternal gargoyle to a little boy.
Cats followed her and she was kind to them.
Lives like hers are blurs of memories like these,
except once – remembered like a bright wing
caught in ancient amber shining like the sun –
when poetry transfigured memory.

One dark night, she woke in fear;
drops, thick and slow, not water, fell on her.
With light she found them golden-red,
oozing spider-webs of gold, dripping
luscious oils from ceiling cracks,
bright honey from the dark attic of her house,
rain of strangeness smearing her white sheets –
generations old and proudly kept – embroidered
with the blood of night-birds in old heraldic tales,
pearls hanging from the open wounds of Saints.

She was a keeper-to-herself,
did not interfere with others' lives
nor wished others to interfere with hers.
But now, the sun just up with singing birds,
she fled her dark and golden house
and came to us to calm her heart,

to tell her story with dramatic hands.
A small boy sat and rubbed his eyes in wonder.
My father acted with concerned despatch.

Mid-morning the bee-catchers came sternly in;
children gathered round in awe
to watch heroic men in masks of black,
stiff yellow canvas suits and leather gloves –
like falconers playing with enormous hawks –
tramp bravely into old Ganteaume's tidy house,
ascend the dark attic to the golden hordes.
There they caught the Queen of the great honey-hive
that all the bright long days had built and burnished.
Then descended, with due ceremony –
to me, transfixed, it seemed with princely step –
casket before them, careful not to let it fall,
(memory tells me it was all of shining gold)
encrusted with golden bees at worship still,
that held the Queen in living, jewelled thrall.
The attic's abandoned bees they smoked to death
in black-winged thousands and swept them out in heaps.
For months old Ganteaume's house with strangeness shone,
fragrance drifting as from the caves of Gods.

A wheelbarrow came over to our house –
somewhere I still hear the axle creak –
filled with cakes of honeycomb,
dripping red, thick heavy drops.
I ate the crisply shining gift of cakes,
heaven's food, sweetness lacing the tongue.
Later huge stars came out in thousands,
seemed to fill the arching sky with light

golden rivers streaming in the night,
stretching without end, a pulsing beauty,
heaven's nearness blazing on the world.

What transmutes the ordinary to other,
as the host-bread baked by sweating men
becomes the living flesh of God?
Men transfixed by poetry,
what first transfixes them?
Memories of love, pain and mind's awakening,
the various beauties that overflow the years,
are not so strong for me as that attic full
of golden bees, the extraordinary honey-spill,
the ropes of sweet, pearled honey-drops,
the bee-encrusted casket of the Queen,
a wheelbarrow arriving at our gate,
creaking, filled with honeycomb –
the golden hives that dripped on old Ganteaume.

Tree of Dreams

I went out and bought a cabbage for supper.
Fire shone in the night.
We bad-talked Dolores and her brood
then I climbed in my tree of dreams.
I got up early and went to work as usual:
golden decisions, morsels of wisdom all day.
At home the left-overs are thrown out
and for all eternity evil is redressed.

Massa Day Done

Viv in a mood today, you only have to watch,
see the jaw grinding, he stabbing the pitch,
    back-lift big.
Look how he stare down the wicket, spear in he eye,
he going to start sudden, violent, a thunder shock.
Man, this could be an innings! This could make
    life good.

You see how he coming in, how he shoulder relax,
how he spin the bat, how he look up at the sun,
how he seem to breathe deep, how he swing
    the bat, swing,
how he look around like a lord, how he chest expan'.
You ever see the man wear helmet? Tell me?
They say he too proud an' foolish.
Nah! He know he worth, boy;
the bowler should wear helmet, not he.
Remember long this day, holy to be here.
See him stalk the high altar o' the mornin' air.

You ever see such mastery in this world?
You ever see a man who dominate so?
This man don't know forbearance,
he don't know surrender or forgive,
he lash the ball like something anger him.
Look how the man torment today!
He holding the bat, it could be a axe.
Look how he grinding he jaw again, boy,
how he head hold cock an' high
and he smile, he gleam, like a jaguar.
Don't bring no flighty finery here; it gone!
Bring the mightiest man, Viv husk he.
He always so, he stay best fo' the best.

I tell you, he smile like he hungry;
you ever see this man caress?
That mood hold he, it bite he!
He pound the ball, look at that, aha!
Like he vex, he slash, he pull, he hook,
he blast a way through the cover, man,
he hoist the ball like cannon ball
gone far and wild, scattering the enemy,
and foe turn tremble, danger all about.
It's butchery today; bat spill blood
and he cut like he cutting hog on a block;
nobody could stop he in that mood.

Almighty love be there! Almighty love, boy.
We know from the start, he one o' we.
Something hurt he bad, you could see,
as if heself alone could end we slavery!

Meeting Once a Year at Britnell's

Which book will I find you browsing in?
"There," you will say, finding the page,
as if no time had passed at all
to wear away life's bright-edged blade a little more.
"When Isaac Singer died he said,
'What the earth swallows is soon forgotten.'
Wrong. 'Like moonlight on whitest sand
we use that dark to gleam, to shimmer.' "

Following a plough through ancient fields
we turn up treasures:
sun-varnished plums that sweeten to the taste.
A Cypriot proverb:
our history is a black stone carved with wings.
Swords shine in Agamemnon's cupboard:
a traveller's fire lit by Gibbon's noble prose.

Still virgin, Newton died at eighty-five.
Was it worth it to discover
the laws of all the universe?
Ah, we have long loved books together
but Walcott's Homer says it well:
"A girl smells better than a book."
No, the poet stands himself corrected,
"A girl smells better than whole libraries."

We have gone long ways apart.
After ferocious evil in the gentle land –
throats gashed to make second mouths of screams,
eyes coldly savaged out of still-fleshed skulls

(Oh, what a work of hate is man!) –
snowfall in Katmandu;
in that far world where mountains climb
gleaming, that age-old, god-filled bastion,
you're safe with love and books and the high stars.

A world away in dark, dazed Guyana,
I settle for the comfortableness of love,
a good wife's caring, the miracle of sons,
a sea-wind murmuring in green trees.
There's well-drawn tea on the veranda,
delicious meat patties melting on the tongue,
jobs to do for money, men from Porlock –
the poetry later, should there still be time.

Let us choose together the spirit's victories:
Mandelstam's widow counting out like gold
word by word his poems in her head –
"The strength of men against cruelty and power
is memory's victory over man's forgetting";
and wisdom's final lesson, and most true –
"He only merits freedom, merits life,
who daily has to conquer them anew."

You told me once:
"We think we are immortal
And we are." It is so still.
Truth does not die and we have savoured it.
The morning's beauty lasts for all its time.

What shall I say, old friend?
Distance, time, still brings no rift.
We sail our separate seas
but when the sea tracks cross
the bright sails unfurled still flash
as I remember, and feel no loss;
the lines that tighten round the mooring post
are strong and taut against the ocean's drift.

The Pear-Wood Cup

Carved pear-wood:
golden as if filled with sun,
cleaned to a shone perfection,
handled to fit a big and battered knuckle,
simple, ordinary, well-proportioned shape,
deep-bowled for a deep thirstiness.
In it the deep, long wear of usefulness,
entering, lasting, then transforming,
has engraved a beauty without passion:
there is no harm in this good thing.
The man who made it lived when times were slow,
knew old occupations that start at morning light.
This cup has no comparison,
no others match it on the kitchen shelf.
In it the touch of generations
joins the taste of everyday:
cold, clear water gets colder, clearer.
The trouble is with us:
too few good things kept safe
come down from the ancestors
to teach us what is past and prized.

Between Silence and Silence There Should Be Only Praise

Should there be a great flood
whole cities would be cast on the fierce water,
floating, drifting, down to an ancient sea;
men and women shouting at the windows,
carrying children to the rooftops,
whimpering in the bleak wind's fury.
Desperate swimming as the houses sink;
life's comfortable arrangements awry and lost.
That slender-waisted girl, sure of her beauty,
she is gone too, with the despots and clowns.
Under the vast sky, much pointless activity –
as well a skull pick its nose and snort
to breathe the evening air.

On the black creek a man's at work;
a fisherman sets a nest of ants afloat,
clump of twigs and green leaves clotted
so intricately to make this insect home,
neat, entangled, well-planned habitation;
now, suddenly adrift, the ant-swarm circles,
tests the water's edge, retreats,
all safety ended.

The impassive fisher sits above;
the floating nest, his subtle bait,
spills ants amidst the swirling flood;
fish flash, gather for the living feast.

He takes his time to flick the rod
assured of victims as the ants drop off
the sinking nest, efficient lure.
The ants' nest drowns and sinks
and bubbles rise like pearls and burst.

Man need not have been. No one knows why
God maintains his kingdom without persuasion:
the dark world of the forest and the river stirs,
intricate catacomb, the grub-furrow under earth
leading to stone, the sun-soar over clouds,
mud-caked Johnny Smallfoot, the bent idiot,
whose pleasant laughter maddens those who sorely
    hurt him.
Shadows pass, empires are cast down.
Friend, it is past the time when tears matter:
between silence and silence, there should be
    only praise.

Birdsong

These are bad days now.
Geometry of the dying mind decrees
zero makes into zero
the enduring primes of life.
It is not the mournful rain
nor the cough deep in the chest
that must be given serious attention
nor the cracks widening in the wall
which must be strongly plastered
nor the unmown grass,
the unraked golden flowers going brown.
The defects again appearing
as they have always appeared
are willingly corrected.
It is not the income and the bills
their measurement and balancing
the habit of dealing with matters as they arise
the responsibility of getting things done
the birthrights, the schooling, the protection
    and the love.
In the fullness of life everything is good,
a wondrous maze of problems and of joys
everlasting harvest of desires.
Now the doing and the doing over
will not have to be done again.
This burst of birdsong is dull.

Silence

I walk here alone among sea-birds:
the graveyard slopes to the sea
a sheet of gold at sunset.
Mahogany trees set against the sun-gold
small green leaves appearing after last week's rain
overhang moss-mottled gravestones
fearsome in their silence.
Solid and serious and unending rock,
they terrify me in their silence.
The sea-birds without motion sway in the wind.
It is a long time since I spoke with those I loved.

Strange Plot

Strange fellowship of the earth,
stones in the graveyard side by side.
The new one brightly cut and shone
for Meg Longstreet died at ninety-three,
and one time-darkened, cracked and crooked,
inscribed for Meg who died at six months old.
She never walked upon this golden earth
nor heard the drum of life go rat-a-tat-tat and boom.
It never ends, through long and fruitful years
the joy, the love, the hope, the good times passing,
the first-born's never-ending loss endures.
"Let me rest by my beloved daughter Meg."

What It Was Like Once Forever

The perfect day is upon me.
I wake to see the gleaming salmon
spring in the dark river of the morning,
the wind full of sea-salt and garden-flower,
the trees brimming slowly with green.
Mongoose, snake-catcher, sleek as a seal,
darts out of sight. I give him a sharp salute.
I give life a salute, the beauty it provides.
The day progresses well, people are well-disposed,
what is owed to business is efficiently transacted.
At home I leap heavenwards as high as I can,
not far but bravely done; my wife smiles,
she shakes her head, after all I am close to seventy-five.
There is no limit to our love,
even death will set no limit.
Our sons are content, healthy as snorting horses,
they will be coming soon.
I write this absurdly happy verse
to tell what it was like once forever.

The Macmillan Caribbean Writers Series

Series Editor: Jonathan Morley

Short Stories:

Crime thrillers:

Fiction:

Plays: